THE IMPORT CAR BUYER'S SURVIVAL GUIDE

JAMES UNDERWOOD

THE IMPORT CAR BUYER'S SURVIVAL GUIDE

E. P. DUTTON   NEW YORK

Published in the United States by E. P. Dutton,
a division of NAL Penguin Inc.,
2 Park Avenue, New York, N.Y. 10016.

Published simultaneously in Canada by
Fitzhenry and Whiteside, Limited, Toronto.

Library of Congress Cataloging-in-Publication Data

Underwood, James.
  The import car buyer's survival guide / James Underwood.—1st ed.
    p. cm.
  ISBN 0-525-48388-8
  1. Automobiles, Foreign—Purchasing. I. Title.
TL162.U53 1988   87-36418
382'.456292'029—dc19   CIP

Designed by Steven N. Stathakis

10 9 8 7 6 5 4 3 2 1

First Edition

CONTENTS

INTRODUCTION

Although there are a number of very informative books on purchasing domestic cars, until now there have been no books especially focused on purchasing imports. Given the fact that there are some drastic differences between the two markets, and that nearly 30 percent of the automotive market consists of import cars, a specialized book is long overdue.

If you're in the market for a new import car, *this book can save you literally thousands of dollars*. Who am I to make such a bold statement? I'm a veteran of six years in the import car business. I've both leased and sold German, Swedish, and Japanese imports in three of the major geographical regions of the country, namely Southern California, the Midwest, and the Northeast. In addition, I worked as the service manager in an import dealership, thereby seeing a side of the business few salesmen ever do. Quite frankly, by the time you've read this book, you will know more about the import car business than most salesmen ever will. You will have been exposed to enough of the "trade secrets" or, more aptly, the "trade differences," to keep yourself from *ever again* paying more than you have to for any new import car you choose to buy. Most assuredly, what I will reveal will prevent me from ever being hired in the business again.

I have made a good living in the import car business, but it's a chapter in my life I've chosen to close. If you are curious about why I would so casually throw it all away, let's just say it's the best way I can think of to perfect my commitment to my new endeavors. This book is nothing short of a bridge burning, one you can profit from.

What you will find in these pages is a detailed, step-by-step, crash course in the realities of the import car market and ways in which even you can prevent yourself from paying too much for your next new car.

You haven't seen this information before. Some of it may make you angry when you find out just how simple it is to avoid the majority of the pitfalls the average buyer encounters in the import dealership. Much of it will run counter to what you thought you knew about buying cars. Be patient. You may not agree with me at first, but by the time we're through you'll be a smarter, better informed buyer than you ever have been before.

Keep in mind that this book deals exclusively with the import car market. If you follow the procedures explained in this book in a domestic dealership you'll be in big trouble; just as much trouble as the poor soul who tries to use domestic-car-buying strategy with the import dealer. If you're after a domestically manufactured car of any description, you'd probably be better off with someone else's book. If that's the case, thank you for the quick look, and best wishes. On the other hand, if you are in the market for an import, you're about to have your eyes opened.

∎ 1

A DIFFERENCE TO BE
RECKONED WITH

Let's start out by clarifying the one simple fact the vast majority of import car buyers, even veteran import car buyers, seem to have missed: domestic and import dealers do not operate the same way. The import supply situation, the selling psychology, and the market slant of the industry are poles apart from the domestic car business we've all grown up with. This means that the technique, the very expertise of the buying public, is ineffective much of the time in the import arena. In short, most of you aren't even vaguely prepared to deal with us, and this means big profits for the dealers and a real likelihood you'll pay more for your new import car than you would if you were only slightly better informed.

But the import dealer isn't invincible. He does have a product in high demand and, like any good businessman, he makes the most of his situation, but he's still very much in a competing mode—import versus import, if not so much import versus domestic—and of course, as in the domestic industry, the competition is just as intense between dealers offering the same make of car. In many ways the car business is the car business; it all looks pretty much the same on the surface. But it isn't the same, and not knowing what the critical differences are can cost you *a tremendous amount of money*.

THE IMPORT ALLOCATION SYSTEM VERSUS DOMESTIC SATURATION

As I found out in six years of selling imports, one of the most fundamental differences between domestic and import dealers has to do with how they get their inventory. If you're a Ford dealer or a Chevy dealer, or whatever, and you want to double the number of cars you have on hand, chances are that a phone call or two, at most, will get the job done, especially if you aren't too concerned with your model mix. You can always count on Detroit to be overstocked with something or other. On the opposite end of the spectrum, if you sell one of the more popular imports, most likely no amount of cajoling will change your situation much.

Import cars are allocated. Who gets what is closely controlled. The various manufacturers may use differing methods, but the bottom line for most dealers is the same: they're only going to get so many cars to sell over the course of a model year.

As an example, I know one Volvo dealer in the Midwest who's had the same allocation for the past thirteen years. He always sells his cars out well before the end of the year. He always asks for more inventory. He never gets it, and he's not unique. The irony in his case, of course, is that not long ago a new Volvo dealership was put in nine miles from his, and *it* has a larger allocation.

Even the Japanese manufacturers, who seem to prefer the more equitable *turn-to-earn* system (meaning that if a dealer sells out, theoretically, he can get an increased allocation the following month), still make it very difficult for a dealer to improve his situation significantly. This, as you can imagine, leads to all kinds of dealer high jinks concerning how many cars get reported sold each month. Creativity, it seems, is far from dead in America.

Among the dealers in the turn-to-earn category, there are indeed a number of "tricks" the dealers employ to fudge their allocations. Because these tricks are so widely practiced, a certain parity exists between dealers, which tends to make the whole routine something of a self-perpetuating farce. Besides which, I can't imagine the distributors as unaware of the games that are being played; this simply flies in the face of logic. The only reason I can think of for the distributors to continue to allow this sleight of hand to go on is that perhaps it supplies them with a certain amount of entertainment. Actually, since no direct harm is done to the consumer, why spoil the fun?

And so the almighty allocation remains the "great carrot" to be held in front of the dealer's nose, and for the obvious reason: if he can get more cars he's simply going to make more money.

From your standpoint what it boils down to is this: for all intents and purposes, the typical import dealer has a fixed number of units from which to generate whatever profit he needs, and he knows what that fixed number is from the very beginning of the model year. This fact probably more than any other tends to temper a dealer's attitude toward discounting. It means he's going to sell you a car for a substantial profit or he's going to wait for the next customer. If he expects to survive and prosper, he has no choice.

You've heard about dealer premiums, availability surcharges, add-on stickers, inflated dealer-preparation charges, mandatory dealer-installed options, and the like. All this comes about when the supply of a desirable product is closely controlled.

Be careful here. What I'm describing is a real land mine for the unsuspecting. The dealer's supply problem quickly becomes your problem. The controlled availability of the import car to the dealer does a number of things beside making the dealer's life more difficult; it's nothing short of the root problem from which the rest of the situation grows. Time and time again you'll be confronted with things that reflect this. Keep your eyes open; know what you're looking at.

WHY THE DEALER WHO HAS MORE PROBABLY GETS MORE

I'm sure you've been to the carnival or circus and that you've seen one of those crazy warped mirrors that make you appear much differently from what you really are. Well, imagine that the allocation system is a sort of warped mirror. If you aren't aware of what you're looking at, you'll get a very distorted idea of the true situation.

For instance, suppose you're out looking for a new car and you come upon a Chevy dealer with four hundred cars on his lot. It's the end of the month. You can see a transporter circling the building looking in vain for a place to unload more cars. To most of us, it's obvious that this dealer will part with one of his units for a minimal profit more easily than a dealer with a half-empty lot. In the domestic business it's a given that the guy with the most cars is probably a discount, or volume, dealer. This individual just calls Detroit, tells them to keep the flood coming, and counts on high numbers rather than the gross profit of each individual sale. Anyone who's ever bought a car is familiar with the scenario.

Surprise! If you're looking at the import lot, the situation could be just the opposite from what you expect, and probably is.

Now I'm going to give something away early here. Even if you don't read the rest of the book, this section will help you save money on your next import car. A large inventory at an import dealership doesn't necessarily mean it either sells more cars or sells them for less. Beware of the import dealer with a larger-than-average inventory, especially at month's end. Usually it means one thing: he's holding his cars until his competition is short on inventory in the hope that he can maximize his profits.

And it works beautifully. You can't effectively comparison-shop when only one dealer has the specific car you're looking for. No matter how much lower another dealer's price is, if he doesn't have the car you want and can't promise you exactly when he'll have it for you, you haven't solved your problem, have you? That's just the idea. To put it in the bluntest possible terms: if I have what you want and no one else does, then you end up buying it for a price I like—that is, a *high* price.

But what about the turn-to-earn allocation system? Doesn't this create a problem for the dealer who's held inventory until the end of the month? Doesn't it lower his allocation for the following month? Theoretically it should, but if the dealer indicates to the manufacturer that all of his units are sold, and if the heldover inventory isn't physically on the dealer's lot for the distributors' spot check, where the factory reps can count the units and adjust the allocations, then the dealer's allocation stands and he can play the game again the following month. (This routine works because the distributor virtually always warns the dealer of an upcoming spot check [or audit, as it's sometimes called] a few days in advance.)

There is a lot of intrigue surrounding this whole issue. Things can become complex in a hurry—just keeping the warranty registrations straight, keeping the bank convinced that you haven't pulled something off on them, making sure the right cars are registered to the right buyers, and so on. But the increased profit to be had by playing this particular game can amount to several hundred dollars per unit. When you're trying to maximize your profit on a very finite number of incoming cars, you learn to live with the complications.

It's incredibly simple: he who has gets, and the procession of unwitting buyers, people who are oblivious to the fact that they're buying with the false conception that a large inventory equates with large discounts in all auto dealers, continues month in and month out.

Take one step forward; you have just removed yourself from this crowd.

THE BUYING SEASON

While we're at it, let's dispel another costly myth. Realize that, chances are, you'll pay more for your new import car at the end of the model year than you would have at the beginning. Yes, you'll get a better deal early in the model year and you'll end up paying more at the end-of-the-year clearance.

There goes my credibility, right? Any neophyte knows that the best deals can be had when the dealer is trying to liquidate his old inventory to make room for the new, right?

Wrong. To begin with, the allocation system exists because the commodity being traded is in short supply. With import cars, supplies are typically shorter at the end of the year than they are earlier. By midsummer the manufacturers have shipped their last current models and have begun to prepare for the new models. The boats still come in for a while—the distributors' holding yards don't empty immediately—but the writing is on the wall, and fairly early.

When supplies get shorter, prices tend to get firmer, and the issue becomes "Can I get the car at all?" not "Can I get the car for my price?" In addition, the yen has risen dramatically in relationship to the dollar recently, which means, at least as far as the Japanese imports are concerned, continued rapidly climbing prices. Four, and sometimes five, price increases have been common over the course of a model year, and some of them can be sharp. I've seen a spread of as much as 12 percent between the manufacturer's suggested retail price at model introduction and that after the last price increase. What does a 12 percent price increase do to a $15,000 car? You've got a calculator; be my guest.

So, even if the dealer does decide to sell a few leftover units at year's end for less than his usual profit margin, chances are the overall price—the only thing that should concern you—will be higher because of the manufacturer's price increases over the course of the year.

If you need a new car, and if your heart is set on an import, don't hang on until the end of the model year. You'll only cost yourself money, and there's the real likelihood the model you've decided on, if you can locate it at all, won't be available in the exact color and level of trim you had in mind. You're going to have to pay for this new car, and it's going to cost you a fair piece of change by anyone's standard. Shouldn't you give yourself the opportunity to get what you want?

DEALER PREMIUMS: WHY PEOPLE PAY THEM; DO THEY MAKE SENSE?

If I've seen it once, I've seen it a thousand times. A car pulls onto the dealer's lot, a man gets out leaving the motor running and the door open, he walks quickly over to the closest car and looks at the price sticker. Suddenly he notices there are two stickers, the manufacturer's sticker and the dealer's add-on sticker. He frowns and moves briskly back to his car and drives off the lot.

If everyone did this, there would be no cars sold for prices over the manufacturer's suggested retail. It simply wouldn't happen. But, of course, the more popular imports are routinely sold for prices in some cases several thousand dollars over the manufacturer's suggested retail. This isn't all Detroit's fault for misjudging their own market. It isn't all because imports tend to be more highly rated than domestics. The highly touted fit, finish, and reliability don't explain the situation in total. Actually, I have seen a few imports being towed down the road on wreckers.

The price of anything isn't set by the manufacturer or the distributor; it's set by the consumer. If a manufacturer or a distributor or a dealer perceives that the public will pay a certain price for his item, he's a fool if he undercuts that figure. If I were working for you in your grocery store and you caught me selling oranges for half price, how long would it take you to fire me? If this book is going to help you, you're going to have to have an accurate idea of the psychology of the dealer. You're going to have to develop an understanding of his thinking in order to cope effectively with him. It is, after all, his game you're going to have to play, and import dealers are in the game to get as much profit as they can from their product. This means they're going to follow the market very closely, and if the market price for any given car exceeds the manufacturer's suggested retail, then some printer somewhere is going to get work supplying additional price stickers.

Angry? Let me take the issue the rest of the way. An add-on sticker, if it represents the true market value of the vehicle it happens to be stuck onto, is more valid than the original sticker anyway. All stickers are arbitrary. But realize this: the add-on sticker is the first and most effective tool a dealer has with which to probe the upper limits of his pricing. If you read the sticker and believe it, he's got you. If you read the sticker and start your negotiations at an artificially high figure because of it, he's got you. In fact, the add-on sticker is such a tremendous tool that the dealer is out of his mind if he doesn't use it to some extent.

By the way, since when is *profit* a dirty word in this country? Why do so many of you think the dealer is immoral because he attempts to sell his product for its market value? If buyers are willing to compete for a product and bid the price up, why should a dealer fight it? Would you?

Now, before you go any further, stop, take a deep breath, and realize the power that you have to deal with this situation.

Who signs your checks? Who makes your decisions? Do you have to buy any particular car from any particular dealer?

What can the dealer do if you don't agree to buy his car? Nothing. All he can do is wait for the next guy to come along and try again. And he isn't nearly as blasé about that prospect as he might have you believe.

To get a clearer picture of this whole add-on price issue, you have to see the additional sticker for what it is: a negotiating tool. Go down to the Ford showroom. You'll see items tacked on to the price of its cars as well. It's just that at a Ford dealership you're less apt to take the sticker seriously. You know that an additional amount can be negotiated away and then some, whether you play games with trade-in allowances, discounts, interest rate buy-downs, down payment percentages, or whatever. The add-on sticker simply allows someone to be a "hero" by supplying a little, albeit often false, working room.

But, especially with imports, some cars are actually sold for over the manufacturer's figure, and no matter who you are or how smart you are, if you choose to buy one of these cars you too will pay the tariff. Of course, even the hottest-selling import has a model or two that staggers a bit in its sales rate, and the dealer isn't going to offer you that information on a platter. He's in the business of getting more per unit, not less, and if you think you have to pay over the sticker for his less popular model, he isn't going to correct you.

So, in the final analysis, some add-on stickers are real and some aren't. The add-on sticker is the first of many smoke screens you're going to have to feel your way through to find the right price on the car of your choice. It's all just part of the game, a game that, until now, you've probably been playing without the benefit of knowing all of the rules.

As long as the public continues to have less-than-satisfactory experiences with what Detroit is producing, and as long as the importers, especially the Japanese, continue to produce cars at a rate that is somewhat short of the demand they enjoy, we're going to be dealing with this "premium" issue.

What I hope to do is show you how you can successfully find the lower limits of the market value on the car of your choice. You won't steal it, believe me, but then again, you won't have to pay over market for it, either.

TAKING A FRESH LOOK
AT WHAT YOU THINK
YOU KNOW

Now that you've discarded some of the more fundamental misconceptions about who you're up against, let's get down to the real business of making you a better player of the game. We'll begin by throwing out some of your most cherished ideas, some of the old standbys that work just fine at Ford or GM or Iacocca's outfit but have a negative value when you play with imports. And we'll go on to focus your attention on the information that will make a difference to you, not only at the time of sale but when you come back in a few years to do it all again.

WHY YOU SHOULD TRASH ALL AVAILABLE
INFORMATION ON DEALER'S COST

The only reason you should ever be concerned with what a dealer pays for his product is if you happen to be considering buying a dealership of your own. I know this may seem to be an outrageous statement, but cost is a nonfunctional piece of information. It's apt to make you unhappy, and it certainly won't help you get a better deal on a car.

Do you suppose the distributor could get a better deal from the manufacturer if he knew what the actual manufacturer's cost of production was? Do you think the dealer would be able to buy cars from the distributor at a more attractive price if he learned what the distributor's markup was? Do you think that McDonald's would sell you a Big Mac for less if you knew what its food cost was? No, of course not, there are too many people waiting in line, willing to pay the price, and if you don't have enough hamburgers to go around in the first place you're certainly not going to give any away.

What is important is the concept of *market* rather than *margin*. This is where you are, like it or not. You aren't going to dictate to a dealer what his "fair" profit should be. Face it, he doesn't care what you think is fair. What he cares about is selling his cars for as much as he knows they will currently bring, and at any given moment a sharp manager will know within a few dollars what that figure is. His game is to improve on that figure: it's the main way a sales manager becomes a general manager. Understand what his motivation is.

Fortunately for you, no dealer can afford to hold his cars forever. Ultimately he has a problem: he runs out of places to hide his inventory from the people who control the allocations. His inventory financing program, commonly referred to as the *floor plan*, exceeds its limits. His salesmen start to migrate to his competition because they're not selling enough cars to support themselves. There rapidly comes a time when greed, excuse me, gross profit per unit, becomes less important than rate of sale and total cash flow. Failure to achieve a balance here is how sales managers become salesmen again, or worse, unemployed.

Here's an axiom for you. No competent sales manager will turn down a deal that falls within what he knows to be the limits of his car's market, even the lower limits.

So put away all of those *Consumer Reports* and *Consumer*

Guide price-and-cost breakdowns and get a firm hold on the real challenge. How do you sound out the lower limits of the actual market on the car of your choice?

WHY YOU SHOULD LEAVE THAT "EXPERT" FRIEND OF YOURS AT HOME

I think all of us have a friend who was in the car business at one time or another; or we know someone who stands around at parties telling stories about how he really raked this or that dealer over the coals; or, just as bad, we know one of those people whose life's work seems to be memorizing the number of spot welds and flat washers in everything from a Yugo to a Ferrari. Do yourself a tremendous favor: get his advice, if you must, *before* you go shopping for your new car. When this individual arrives at the dealership, he's interested in only one thing—justifying his presence. He wants to prove to you just how valuable he is, and he generally ends up obstructing the entire process.

He'll begin by asking technical questions about models you have no interest in whatsoever. He'll try to demonstrate just how much he knows and how little the pitiful car salesman knows. He'll mire you down in long-winded dissertations that will sound impressive but have no bearing on what you're trying to accomplish with your visit to the dealership.

Car salesmen get played with twelve hours a day, seven days a week, by customers, by sales managers, by service managers, and by other salespeople. You don't want to play games with a veteran. By now he's too good at it for you, and what's worse, it's a waste of your valuable time. Who cares what the salesman knows about the technical workings of his product? *Road and Track, Car and Driver, Autoweek,* the federal government's crash test results, *Consumer Reports,* and your local independent mechanic, all have the advantage of not trying to sell you any particular car. They simply supply information, some good, about cars, and the best part is that they don't interrupt you as you're trying to get your business done. Get your hard, technical information from these people—it's their business.

You shouldn't go to a dealership to talk about cars, anyway; you should go to a dealership to find out about buying a car. And what you should find out from the salesman has to do with availability, advance notifications of price increases, cars in stock, hard-to-get colors or models, the specific makeup of his next incoming allocation, and so on. Ask him about the things he knows best, and he'll help you.

No one knows your automotive needs as well as you do. What's infinitely better to bring to the dealership, instead of your "expert" friend, is a clear idea of what particular needs this car has to fill. Give it some thought beforehand. You're the one who knows how big the backseat needs to be because of your full-figured mother-in-law. You're the one who is six-foot-two and needs extra room in the driver's seat. More than once I've seen people have arguments with their "expert" friends right on the showroom floor over what kind of car to buy. It's a natural reaction for someone to become upset when you ask for their advice and then don't take it. Why would you want to put a friend in that position?

There is a place and a time for your friend, but it isn't now. If he's insistent, have him take you to an auto show, and suggest that you'll buy the tickets. You'll be way ahead of the game.

QUESTIONS YOU SHOULDN'T HAVE TO ASK YOUR SALESPERSON

Notice that in my little laundry list of items you should ask your salesperson about, I didn't mention payments. This wasn't an oversight; I left it out on purpose. The man or woman you're talking with is a professional negotiator and also a professional number handler. There are computers nowadays, the size of a normal calculator, that are programmed to give the salesman a wealth of information that is instantly beneficial to him and totally misleading to you. He can even turn that little computer around and let you see it, if he's clever, and you've been sunk without even knowing it. I'll cover the majority of these little maneuvers in the chapter about loans, but for now I'd like to introduce you to the basics of something I call *covert* negotiation, because that's exactly what it is.

We're all payment buyers to some extent. Even the individual who pays cash is a payment buyer, albeit a one-payment buyer. The normal situation is that we judge how expensive an item is by what it does to our monthly budget. To the vast majority of us, however, the relationship between purchase price and monthly payment is fuzzy at best. Even the people who take the initiative and try to figure payments beforehand with a pocket calculator invariably do it wrong. It's so much easier to sit back in the salesman's nice, comfortable chair, sip his free coffee, and let him tell you what the payments will be. Fortunately for the salesman, and for the dealership, most people do just this.

The problem is that what you don't know about can too easily be misrepresented. If you put yourself in the position of having to depend on the salesman to tell you what your payments will be, there are a dozen ways he can work this to his advantage—and none that work to yours.

But the price is the price, you say; how can you misrepresent that? Easy. Let me ask you this: is the price going to change downward during our negotiations? You don't buy a car, usually, unless it does, do you? Suppose for a moment I initially quote payments on a loan amount higher than the one you would actually need. Are you going to be aware of what I did? Probably not. Now, as we negotiate, if I adjust my payments downward at an artificially accelerated rate, will you catch on to what I'm doing? Will you detect the "cushion"

I'm maintaining, or will it appear that you're really making headway and that I'm negotiating in good faith and sincerely reaching for your business? Chances are that I actually have picked up a little goodwill with this little ruse, but this is only window dressing. What else have I accomplished for myself?

People in this country have learned a tactic called "split the difference." What I've gained from my little game is that most likely I've given myself several opportunities, based on payments, to split the difference with you, in my favor, without your being aware of what's actually happened. With the negotiations focused on payments and little attention being paid to the exact price being used as a factor, how do you know where your negotiations really are?

With no accurate way to figure payments for yourself, the only way you can protect yourself from this tactic is to keep the negotiation centered squarely on price alone. The disadvantage, of course, is that you may not have any idea how your price equates to your budget. People often commit themselves to things they really can't afford.

So the answer must be to insist that price and payments be quoted side by side, right? Better, but still not safe. You still don't know whether the two numbers accurately relate to each other. The payment could still be based on a higher figure, and this opens the door for a second type of covert negotiation—namely, the opportunity for someone in a separate profit center, further down the delivery process, to come in and very painlessly sell you something additional, such as an extended warranty, or rustproofing, or paint sealant, or whatever.

If you agreed to buy the car, it's obvious you've been preconditioned to a monthly figure. You've accepted it; you're comfortable with it. Now let me ask you this: are you more apt to buy something that increases your payment by $1 or $2, or something that increases your payment by $20? There is potential here for you to spend money you didn't even know you had. Something to think about, isn't it?

We'll discuss this area more later, but for now I simply want to be sure you understand how important it is for you to know how to figure your own payments. There's a gap in most people's logic here. The first thing they want to see for themselves when they get to the dealership is the exact price, in black and white, on the window sticker. They won't take the slightest chance that the salesman might quote an inflated price to them. Why would these same people even consider taking that same salesman's unsubstantiated word for the payments? At this point, it should make as little sense to you as it does to me.

A PRACTICAL AMORTIZATION TABLE

Have you ever seen an amortization table? Usually it consists of rows and rows of tiny numbers designed in such a way that you have to depend on the banker to read it to you. For that reason I'm not going to republish someone else's table; that would only confuse the issue. What I am going to do is give you a tool that will give you a reliable feel for what your payments should be at any given loan amount for the most popular loan terms, 48 and 60 months. Fair warning, though: don't try to fill out a bank contract or second-guess someone's computer down to the last few cents with it. This is a method for you to use under fire, when you're excited and under pressure to make a decision; it's designed to be simple so you can use it right when it counts. It's only accurate enough to serve this purpose.

I suggest that you buy the cheapest pocket calculator you can find. For heaven's sake, don't bring in your two-zil-lion-K-memory home computer or even one of the scientific, programmable things. You'll only open up the opportunity to make a mistake. Besides, you want to look like regular people to your salesman, not like someone he doesn't want to spend his time on.

▪ ▪ ▪

Here's the procedure:

At 10 percent interest, a $1,000 loan requires a little over $25 a month on a 48-month loan. Write the following equation on a small piece of paper and tape it to the back of that new calculator.

48-month loan
1.thousand* x 25 =

Now suppose you'll be financing $8,000. The equation operates like this:

8 x 25 = $200 per month.

Suppose the loan amount is $12,500?

12.5 x 25 = $312.50 per month.

If the actual loan amount is $12,513, and you have an insatiable appetite for accuracy, you could do this:

12.513 x 25 = $312.83 per month.

But you don't really need to be that specific.

You get the idea, I'm sure; just replace the comma in the loan amount with a decimal point and multiply by 25 for your payment amount, rounding off the numbers to whole dollars.

What about 60 months? Get another small piece of paper and more tape and write this down for the back of your calculator.

60 months
1.thousand x 21 =

How about a $9,400 loan?

9.4 x 21 = $197.40 per month.

---

*No, don't put the zeros in in place of the word *thousand*; I've expressed the equation this way for a reason. And yes, I meant to put a decimal point after the number 1.

A $14,900 loan?

14.9 x 21 = $312.90 per month.

Go ahead and practice with this until you're sure of what you're doing. Don't wait until you're in front of a salesman to learn how. A little repetition at this stage goes a long way toward making you bulletproof.

Now let's discuss accuracy. Obviously, this method isn't dead accurate. I've done some streamlining for the sake of simplicity. (Using the formula given, the payment you'll come up with for a $10,000 loan based on 10 percent interest and a 48-month term will be low by about $4.10. The payment for the same loan but with a 60-month term will be low by about $2.50.) The ability to determine quickly what your monthly payment should be, within a couple of dollars, puts you way ahead of the fellow who's totally at the mercy of his salesman.

Answer this question for me. If you sat down with me now and I quoted a payment that was $50 too high, would I be able to get away with it as easily? Would anyone's attempt to employ a little covert negotiation on you run into a problem at this point? Have you just become a smarter customer?

That's fine, but we're still not finished. There's still an opportunity for a salesman to tell you that your figures are off because you aren't figuring your payments based on the right interest rate. There's still a chance for a smart salesman to insert a little fog between you and the real figures.

Let's take a look at what a change in interest rate actually does to a monthly payment. Our initial $8,000 loan for 48 months had a $200 monthly payment. Suppose instead of 10 percent interest the actual rate was 8 percent? Instead of a factor of 25 you would have to use a factor of 24, and your equation would become:

8 x 24 = $192 per month.

or an $8.00-per-month difference for a 2 percent change in

interest rate. If you increase the interest to 12 percent, your factor becomes 26.

$$8 \times 26 = \$208 \text{ per month.}$$

The same $8.00, or, if you want, an adjustment of $4.00 a month per each 1 percent change in interest rate.

Is it really this simple? For your purposes it is. To bring your estimated monthly payment into line with the actual interest rate, adjust your figures by $4.00 per each whole percentage point up or down. Just keep in mind that the further away you get from our baseline of 10 percent the greater the variation from absolute accuracy there is in the method. Be that as it may, the fact remains that you now have some reasonable way to relate purchase price to monthly payment, and that's the whole idea for my amortization table.

WHY APPEARING TOO SMART IS REALLY DUMB

We touched on this in the last section, but it deserves expansion. Just as there are covert and overt negotiation tactics the dealer employs, there are covert and overt counternegotiation tactics you can and should employ.

Don't misunderstand me, I don't suggest you do or say anything dishonest or even misleading in order to negotiate effectively with the dealer. Just the opposite—you're going to win on the basis of good information, not subterfuge.

What I am saying is that when you discover a dealer in the act of one of his covert little ploys, you'll find that often the most powerful and beneficial thing you can do is say nothing, even when the dealer is doing something so flagrant it's comical. Stay calm and simply keep making the right decisions. *Your* most powerful covert tactic is in knowing what is going on without the salesman's being aware of your knowledge.

If you sense that the payments are being quoted with a cushion, don't accuse your salesman of being underhanded.

You gain nothing by showing him how smart you are; besides, he might just be following the instructions of his manager or the policy of the dealership. This salesman may still produce the lowest price you can find. He may still be the best person to deal with. Let him try his tactics; so much the better if you recognize what he's up to. Keep on playing the game until you get what you want. That's what you're there for, not a confrontation.

Don't burst onto the showroom floor waving your brand-new five-dollar calculator in the air and shouting "No one's going to pull one over on me, by God!" No dealer is going to suddenly change his system for you. You aren't going to intimidate him into dropping the tactics that have made him a wealthy person. But if you maintain a nice low profile and make the preparations I'm going to show you, you will slip through his system quite effectively.

One more thing. Human nature applies to the salesman, his manager, the general manager, the dealer principal (fancy name for owner), and everyone you come in contact with at the dealership. Everyone prefers to work with someone who's reasonable. You want them to make an investment of their time in you willingly. You want them to think that they can sell you a car. You don't want them to be glad when you walk out. When they start to value you as a customer, you move closer to their minimum-profit deal.

From the very beginning, just as a salesman and his sales manager try to pigeonhole you by what they think you're apt to buy and what you're apt to pay for it, you must determine what kind of games the dealer and the salesman and the sales manager are likely to play. Detecting a maneuver isn't something to be upset about; it's something to file away in your information bank. It's something that will save you money and time later on.

So don't come on too smart. Learn to play good defense.

A MATTER OF EMOTION WHEN IT SHOULD BE A MATTER OF LOGIC

You have to be pretty far along into *rigor mortis* before the prospect of a shiny new car fails to get your blood pumping. For some people, cars are almost pure emotion and, whether or not you fall into this category, you must realize that emotion is a dangerous pitfall for all of us. If only the birth control pill had a corollary in the automobile business! Unfortunately, it doesn't. Lose your head over an automobile and you will suffer the consequences.

There's a lot to be said for owning a car that you like, one that excites you and adds a little something to the quality of your existence. Getting emotionally involved with a neat car can be—and is, for a lot of people—great fun and perfectly logical.

What isn't such great fun, if you aren't careful, is finding out you've ruptured yourself financially, after the fact. Contrary to popular dogma, you can still lose your shirt on the most popular models of the most popular imported cars, the ones with the supposedly highest resale value. The act of buying an import does not magically immunize you from waking up some morning and finding that you owe more money on your loan than your car is worth.

You must induce yourself to buy a car that meets at least your most important needs and one that you can afford. You have to force yourself to look into the future a bit and determine how you will fare with any given car you may be considering buying. There are many absurd examples I could cite of people who failed utterly in this regard, but it's too depressing. Use the darkest corners of your imagination and you won't be far off.

There's a very colorful term in the car business: *upside-down Charlie*. This is what you're called if you attempt to trade in a car that fails to appraise for more than your loan balance. Often people who fall into this category are trading in the first year or two of a 60-month loan that was arranged with a small down payment, or they're attempting to terminate a lease early, or they've done something to their car that has depreciated its value faster than normal (extremely high mileage, for instance, or unrepaired mechanical or body damage). But it's also possible to be in the third or fourth year of a lease or a purchase and still be faced with the problem. You can make your car unfit for human operation at any point, early or late. You might have allowed yourself to be "buried" in your new car as a result of some "creative" refinancing of a portion of the unpaid loan balance of your previous car. There are a lot of ways you can be engineered into this position, and unless you don't mind being a walking repossession just waiting to happen, you'd better take a close look at some of the fundamentals of avoiding the problem.

HOW TO AVOID EVER BECOMING AN UPSIDE-DOWN CHARLIE

Are you familiar with financial projection? It's what a businessman does to make sure he's prepared for upcoming expenses: a larger factory, or a new piece of equipment, or more employees. Well-developed projections are always at the root of good planning.

Happily, projecting what your new car will be worth at any given point in your ownership of it is extremely simple. The wholesale and retail values of used cars are among the most highly documented figures there are, probably because so much money changes hands over used cars in this country each year. Fortunately, this information is readily available to anyone, not just the dealers.

Call them Kelly Blue Books, NADA (National Automobile Dealers Association) price guides, or whatever, but they're around. Your banker has one. Your library might even have one. Every dealer in the known world has several. Pick someone you're reasonably comfortable talking to and do a little research.

You say the book looks complicated? It is. That's why I'm going to suggest that if it's possible you sit down with the loan officer at your local bank and let him read it to you. He'll be impressed with your good sense, which won't hurt your loan application later, and in the short run you'll have more confidence in your information.

There are, however, some questions you'll want to have answers to beforehand. These questions constitute square one in this procedure.

How long did you keep your present car? How many miles did you drive it? Is there anything in your situation that you know will change during the next few years, such as a new job that will require more driving? Use common sense. Make a profile of what the mileage and condition of your car is likely to be. Do you travel with large dogs? Do you have unruly children who like to puncture your upholstery? We're talking about your money here, so be honest.

You already know what you're going to do next. You're going to take the same make and model car, or as close to it as you can get, and see what a three-, four-, or five-year-old version is worth today. Most books are kind enough to list the original manufacturer's retail price, so simply take the figure you come up with (don't forget to use the mileage tables) and subtract it from the original price. Do it for wholesale and for retail. Now convert the change in value to a percentage. Apply this percentage to the sticker price of the new car, less any dealer add-ons, and you have an instant projection of what your new car should be worth, at least in the book, when you get ready to trade or to sell it privately. Next, look across the desk and ask your banker where you would be with your proposed loan at your estimated point of trade.

When you've completed this projection, you may be startled with the result, but it's far better to be startled now than at the time of trade. While the realization of just how expensive this new car of yours is going to be is still turning your stomach over, pardon me for making things worse for you.

I've never seen a car traded in where the real value accredited to it was anywhere near "book" value. There are always adjustments made to compensate for rough condition, bad tires, deferred maintenance, smelly upholstery, funny colors, and above all current wholesale market conditions. In trade-ins what you see is most assuredly not what you get.

We'll go into more detail in Chapter 7, which discusses trade-ins, but for now what I want you to do is make a "worst-case" set of numbers for yourself. Take your projected trade-in value and reduce it by 20 percent.

Now you have a figure to use in your planning that will keep you from getting hurt in almost any eventuality.

WHY MOST NEGOTIATING "TIPS" MISS THE POINT ENTIRELY

Out of a well-developed sense of self-preservation as a salesman, I've read most of the books that have been written claiming they contain secret and powerful "tips" on how to beat the dealer at his own game. Some explain how to figure the dealer's cost, the uselessness of which we've already covered. Others offer the peculiar advice that you should lie to the dealer and tell him you can buy his car elsewhere for a very low figure, apparently with the idea in mind that he'll immediately drop to a subminimum gross profit deal in order to get your business away from the "other" dealer. I've always thought this strange, but then I've always sold imports and most books of this type are slanted toward the domestic buyer. The truth is that at the average import dealership misrepresenting the prices you've been quoted is going to do little more than embarrass you. Import dealers don't sell cars for less than the market because their inventory, unlike the domestic variety, is too hard to replace. What's more, the import dealer knows that his competition shares the same attitude. (Some dealers do tend to gravitate toward either the upper or lower end of the market, and identifying which is which is, of course, one of the main topics of this book.)

At my last dealership, if you walked onto the showroom floor and gave a false price to virtually any of the salesmen, he would undoubtedly see it for what it was (unless, of course, you got very lucky and happened to guess correctly, which isn't likely). The difference is this: the community of import dealerships is very small in comparison to the large number of domestic dealerships. It's like living in a small town. Everybody pretty much knows what everybody else is up to. Drop a price that's phony and all you're doing is telling the salesman you haven't shopped. You've also destroyed your credibility, which is worse.

Lying to the dealer never gets you into the lower levels of the market on his car; having the right information at the right dealership always does. Give a competent import salesman a real price (naturally, from one of his competing dealers selling the same make), and he will probably tell you where you got that price and also whether that dealer actually has that specific car in stock. I'm not saying this to intimidate you. I'm merely trying to point out the disservice you do yourself by trying to bluff your way through the process.

There is no substitute for the right information.

Another equally silly notion is that you should lead the dealer to believe you're going to arrange your financing through him and then at the last moment pay cash or present a check from your own bank. The rationale seems to be that the dealer can be lulled into loading his profits into his loan package and be caught when you unexpectedly make other arrangements.

The import dealer does want to do the financing for you. He does make money from the loans he arranges, but each unit sold must maintain a gross profit exclusive of any additional revenues from the sale. The "quick switch" at the end of the deal won't accomplish anything but screw up your paper-work at the time of delivery. If you plan to have your own financing arranged outside of the dealership, which is the way to go in most cases, tell the dealer up front.

You may be tired of my saying this by now, but you aren't going to trick the dealer into selling you a car for less than its market value. What you *can* do is keep him from tricking you into paying more than its market value. Most negotiating tips I've seen simply aren't valid.

A dealer has no trick, or ploy, or tactic, that will work against a buyer who knows the market value of the product in question. The dealer's game is over the moment you know the right set of numbers. The way to win is to learn how to comparison-shop effectively so you can discover that right set of numbers.

▪ 3

COMPARE TO WIN

Have you ever watched a gifted magician work? When you're under the spell of a true master his illusions can easily be accepted as fact; his showmanship is thoroughly convincing. This is the level all magicians strive for: total credibility in the eyes of an audience. Because of these individuals, for a moment, we believe in magic; for a moment, we allow ourselves to ignore hard facts. Somewhere in the back of your mind you know the magician isn't telling you the truth, but, at the critical moment, you allow the force of his performance to override your common sense.

The magician, as it turns out, knows a secret about human psychology that helps him with his craft. He knows that we all subconsciously *want* to believe in magic. For some reason we seem to want to be fooled. It's easier to believe in magic than it is to figure out what's really happening.

I've always thought that the automobile salesman has a good deal in common with the magician. Each tries to present a situation in a way that's convincing. Each is trying to conceal certain elements of his performance from an attentive onlooker. Each at his most astute is a consummate showman. We applaud the magician's illusions; after all, they're benign. But in the automobile salesman's case, illusions can cost you money. Obviously, you have a good reason to guard against being overcome by this individual's performance.

Separate the illusion and the showmanship from the hard facts and what you have left might not be terribly entertaining, but it will be the truth. The truth is the only thing that will keep you from spending a lot more money on your new car than you have to.

There are what amount to a *long course* and a *short course* in this business of survival in the import car market. If all you want to do is to pay somewhere in the middle of the bracket of market value for the car of your choice, then simply scout the dealers in your area for the one who seems to sell his cars out before anyone else does each month. Or order your car early from the dealer with the longest waiting list. Or pick a time early in the year, when all of the dealers in your area have a fairly substantial inventory, to buy your car. Any of these tactics will tend to moderate what you have to pay for your new car. Just avoiding the most flagrant of the holdouts—easy enough to identify because they always seem to have cars even when supplies are generally short—will do you substantial benefit. So much for the short course.

To get into the lower areas of market value, however, you're going to have to invest some time and effort. This is the long course, and it's more than a little time-consuming, frustrating, and challenging. But if you're still game, you're about to learn how to get the total available discount.

WHY SPECIFICS ARE EVERYTHING

First, you have to decide what you want. Don't even think about collecting price information until you're satisfied with what kind of a car meets your needs functionally, economically, and egotistically. The onset of price negotiation is like a closet door. Behind it, poised to tumble out on you, are all of the little tricks and strategies dealers like to use to commit you to buying a car before you're ready. Keep that door completely shut until you've kicked your quota of tires.

Go on demo rides. Look under hoods. Read the brochures. Study the magazines. Listen to the salesman's presentation of his product. But make it clear from the beginning that you are not ready to ask for a price. Tell him honestly that when you decide what kind of a car you want you'll be back to discuss what he might be able to do for you.

Fair warning: once your intentions are clear, some salesmen won't spend any time at all with you. They won't even give you a fundamental explanation of what models they have to offer. They'll turn their back on you, find something else to do that suddenly can't be put off, try to turn you over to one of the new guys so he can practice on you. Fine. Don't be put off. You're better off with the least experienced salesman you can find, anyway. If your "old pro" chooses to ignore you, so much the better. It only gives you the opportunity to look the product over without the distraction of having to joust with someone experienced who's intent on getting you to commit to a sale on the spot.

Of course, you may run into someone who's adept at laying traps and snares and who's willing to take a shot at you. If so, be polite—and be firm: no prices today.

As a salesman, I've always hated role-playing. It's like going duck hunting with blanks. You can go through the motions, but there's no payoff, not even if you know your shot would have been a direct hit. Here are a few lines, however, that may help you stay out of trouble.

Q: Sir, how do you know if this car fits your budget if you don't at least investigate what it can be bought for?
A: According to the window sticker, it fits my budget. I just don't know if it's the car I want.
Q: If there were a way I could save you some substantial

money on this particular car, would you consider at least talking about price?

A: You seem to be interested in my business. Would you show me some of the features of your car instead?

Q: Do you have a trade-in you'd like us to appraise today?

A: No.

Do you like the last answer? I do. Sometimes offering the smallest amount of information you can works to your advantage. A simple, straightforward, very politely spoken no is a very difficult hurdle for a salesman to clear. It never sounds contrived or "canned," and it's an easy line to deliver with sincerity. If you can't redirect your salesman back onto the topics you've come to talk about, don't be afraid to stop him with a simple no. After a while he'll get the idea and become concerned with damaging his rapport with you.

Even though the car business is very much a "today" business, any salesman knows he has to sell a car tomorrow as well. Eventually you'll get your way.

The task you must remain focused on for now is developing a specific shopping list. The more detailed the better, but simplicity has its virtues. What I'm having you do is draw a baseline to operate from. Everyone in the world is going to try to confuse the issue, so you should start out with a clear idea of what is really important to you.

Don't go overboard on simplicity, though. If you know you'll need air-conditioning, put it on your list. If you know you want the factory stereo system, write it down (exact model descriptions, please!).

Then, once you know about the hardware, turn your attention to the software. Go home, get a pencil, a calculator, a telephone, and whatever personal budgeting information you use.

Be very specific about money. Know what monthly payments you can handle. Play with the amortization equation I've given you and get a feel for how large a loan that payment equates to. Make some calls and find out what the current situation is on interest rates. Adjust your factors ahead of time.

Decide what your time frames are. How soon do you need the new car? Do you need the best deal you can find on a car that's in stock now? Or could you wait a few weeks for one to show up on someone's incoming allocation? Make these decisions now, on your own, so the salesman doesn't make them for you.

One of the most common, and also one of the most costly, mistakes the average buyer makes is to show up at a dealership not knowing what he wants. Then he attempts to do everything in one fell swoop. He decides model, color, number of doors, in-stock or incoming, where he's going to get his financing, what monthly payments he can afford, whether or not to buy an extended warranty, and so on.

No matter who you are or what your qualifications are, it's just too much for you to do effectively in one sitting. Before long you get tired and confused and start to make bad decisions. You also spend far too much time with the salesman. You tend to start seeing him as a friend and adviser. It's simple human nature; you let your guard down. You think: Gee, I really don't want to go through all of this three or four more times. I'll just ask for his best deal and buy the car today.

Don't make this more difficult for yourself than it is. It just doesn't make sense to give yourself a handicap you can avoid. Opening price negotiations when you've established ahead of time what your specific parameters are puts you several steps ahead of the average customer. Why not give yourself the opportunity to play this game in top form?

HOW TO COMPARE SAME TO SAME IN SPITE OF THE GIMMICKS

When you've narrowed your search down to one make of car, and one particular model of that make, and you've decided what accessories you need, and when you've decided what monthly payments make sense to your situation, *then and only then* are you ready to start collecting price information. This is going to be an adventure. Even though you will consistently ask for a price quote on exactly the same model with exactly the same equipment at each dealership you go to, you won't get a straightforward quote anywhere. The dealers are much too smart for that. Comparison shopping costs them far too much money for them to make it easy for you. You'll find "packages" included at some dealerships that become separately purchased items at others. You'll find some salesmen who can handle extended warranties at the desk and others who'll pass you on to a different person. You aren't going to be able to go into three or four dealerships, get a sealed bid, take them all home, and find out who the winning supplier is. If that were the case, there would have been no need for me—or anyone else, for that matter—to write this kind of book.

The reason dealer principals keep pesky salesmen around, instead of a row of nice, neat vending machines, is to complicate your life and increase the gross profit of their deals.

Remember our magician friend and his illusions? Packages are the salesman's illusions. You will be led to believe that this or that package is worth big money. You'll also discover that each dealer has a different package. They do this sort of thing on purpose to fog the issue for the comparison shopper. A Honda Accord LXi is the same Honda Accord LXi at whatever dealership you go to. Like most imports, this car is highly standardized. The manufacturer does this to streamline his actual manufacturing process (or *build out* as it's called), simplify his quality control, and maximize his production. It creates a problem for the dealer, though. It makes his cars too easily comparable. The domestic dealer can have eight zillion slightly different versions of the same model; some with tilt-wheel, some without, some with talking computers, whatever. The import dealer is forced to be creative if he intends to protect his profit structure.

Needless to say, you won't get very far in your price comparisons unless you have an idea what these packages are really worth. Let's start off by talking about one of the most popular items to be included in a package: the extended warranty.

An extended warranty is commonly provided to the dealer by a supplier other than the manufacturer. It's nothing more than an insurance policy, insuring against the possibility of mechanical breakdown. There are hundreds of different policies offered by a wide range of companies, but they share one common denominator: you pay a premium, based on the demonstrated reliability of your particular make of car. Simply put, the more troublesome the car in question has proved to be, the higher the cost of the warranty. An insurance company calls this *underwriting the risk*.

The customer, however, might never guess that there has been any sort of studied comparison drawn between different makes and models of cars. The last thing the dealer wants to give you is yet another method of rating his products. (Too bad; this one would be extremely reliable, for the obvious reason that insurance companies hate to lose money.) What the dealer does is charge what he feels the traffic will bear with no thought given to the subtleties of the warranty company's rate card.

A fifty-thousand-mile, five-year extended warranty on a highly rated car will seldom cost the dealer more than $150. Even so, I've seen dealers routinely charge their customers anywhere from $200 to $600 for the same coverage.

If you live anywhere in the snow belt, another item of great interest is rustproofing. The materials used to rustproof the average car cost the dealer about $25. The labor is usually done by one of the junior cleanup men whose hourly rate probably hovers just over minimum wage. Your new car might take thirty-five to forty minutes to rustproof. The dealer's retail cost to his customer? Anywhere from $200 to $400.

An item that sells well in the warm climates is a solution

that is sprayed over cloth upholstery to protect it from sun fade and various types of spills and stains. Cost? About $15 to $20 tops, and maybe a half hour's worth of labor. Dealer's retail? In the range of $75 to $150.

Paint sealant is another extra, this one with coast-to-coast appeal. I have seen one process that cost the dealer about $100, but most fall well below $50, including labor. Dealer's retail? At least $100 to $300.

Most people don't realize that they are paying a 300 or 400 percent markup on what they're buying. This is one of the real power points of the package. These extras can be made to seem as if they're worth a lot—and they are, to the dealer.

There are two things for you to consider. First, these after-market products have some value; you may *want* an extended warranty, rustproofing, or paint sealant. But if you know you want an after-market product, negotiate for it as part of your deal. Have it included in the price up front. If you have to see someone else in the dealership in order to buy what you want, the dealer is attempting to split his profit centers on you. Suddenly you'll find yourself in a new game with a fresh player.

The salesman and his manager are motivated to make their deal. If they have to give away some of another department's money to do it, they just might go right ahead and take the heat for it later. They have their gross profit target number clearly in mind, and if they have to include a warranty at cost to make you an owner, they may chose to.

Once you're out on the road with your new car, if you come back for rustproofing or some item the service department or parts department has to be involved with, you, of course, have another set of players to contend with.

Second, the further removed you become from the initial negotiation for the purchase of your new car, the more expensive any additional items will become. (I used to give away a little leather key chain to my customers that I later found out the parts department was charging $11 for. As I have a perverse sense of humor, I continued to give them away.)

Now we come to the financing gimmicks. Chapter 5 is devoted to loans and financing, but I want you to realize that financing can be the most difficult of all the gimmicks for you to evaluate, especially if you have no way to figure payments. The key to evaluating the various artificially lowered rates is to compare actual total of payments. Some of these programs make sense now that we have a brand-new tax law that virtually eliminates the interest deduction. However, be careful to base your comparisons on a same-to-same basis. And keep in mind that the extra sales price you usually end up paying because of these programs carries with it a nondeductible sales tax, courtesy of the same law.

Heaven help you if you base your comparisons totally on salesman-supplied information. When in doubt, call time-out, go home, and make sure you know what you're doing.

I hope this section helps you when you get home and lay out all the different combinations of prices and packages. Don't be discouraged if it takes you some time to analyze what you have in front of you. If it makes you feel any better, keep in mind that it is the end product of the work of a pretty sharp group of professional complicators.

Just don't make the mistake of attaching too high a value to the packages that will be shoved at you. Include the items you want, by all means, but disregard what you really don't want in your value comparisons. At some point, things will begin to make sense.

THE MYTH OF THE *ORDERED* CAR

When you're sitting at the dealership, you aren't dealing with the manufacturer. When the dealer buys cars, he isn't dealing with the manufacturer either. Only the distributor deals directly with the manufacturer. There is no direct connection between the retail sales order you may have just signed and what actually gets built at the factory. This might not be true if you were dealing with the ultra-high-priced specialty cars such as Ferrari, Lamborghini, Rolls-Royce, or the like, but it is true with virtually all of the "mass-produced" imports: German, Swedish, Japanese, Yugoslavian, and Korean. If this disturbs you, it should. It means your order will be filled on a catch-as-catch-can basis.

During the preceding model year, the manufacturer has canvassed his distributor for advice on the breakdown of the build out—how many of what and in what color the manufacturer should produce. This is the only time the distributor and his dealer network have any direct input to the factory. It's the only time the manufacturers' ears seem to be open. Once the percentages and subpercentages are set, that's it. If Honda decides to build only 15 percent of the model run as Preludes and only 5 percent of that figure in black, any orders that are still around after those cars are built simply don't get filled. Honda isn't going to build one more black Prelude for anyone.

The situation isn't any different with Toyota, or Nissan, or Volvo, or Audi, or Volkswagen. Why? Don't they realize they could sell more cars if they gave the public exactly what it wanted?

Yes and no.

You see, you folks buy every car they can get away with sending over here anyway, so why should they change their program just because one librarian in Butte, Montana, happened to take the last Toyota Celica Supra that was available, and you're left holding a worthless, unfilled order? They couldn't care less if you have to wait until next year. Chances are they'll only make more money on the unit in question when they actually do get around to building it, given price increases and the falling value of the dollar.

Is it a sham, then, to order a car from a dealer? No, but

you have to have a realistic idea of what's possible and what isn't. You have to redefine what the word *order* means in "import-car-ese."

When you order a car, the first thing a dealer does is look at his incoming monthly allocation, if he happens to have that information at the moment. I don't think the distributors themselves know what the manufacturer is loading onto the boats until the last moment, so how can he tell the dealer what he'll be getting very far in advance? If he comes up empty on his own allocation, he calls his fellow dealers and tries to arrange a trade with someone who does have what he needs. It's like reaching into a big grab bag and hoping. If the dealer keeps reaching and hoping long enough, he connects. Sooner or later, if the buyer's patience doesn't run out, or if the manufacturer doesn't reach the end of his planned build out, or if the dealer doesn't exceed the number of those cars allocated to him, the car gets delivered to the happy new owner. Let's hope it comes off the truck without too much damage, though, because if it does everyone goes back to square one.

THE REAL DIFFERENCE BETWEEN *IN STOCK, INCOMING,* AND *LOCATE*

From our discussion above, you can see now that the status of your "ordered" car is something you should pay attention to. If it's sitting right there on the lot, where the cleanup people can get their hands on it, that's one thing. If no one has the faintest idea of where your car is, or when it will appear at the dealership, that's obviously something entirely different.

If you're attempting to compare prices among cars that fall into different categories, you need an accurate understanding of how the subtleties of differing availability bear on price.

Replace the words *in stock* with *real* in your vocabulary. Your price on an in-stock vehicle is more than likely real, at least at the moment. It's also probably a higher price than the best you could get. Let me explain.

If a dealer has inventory when no one else does, it's because the shoppers found his prices higher than what they could get elsewhere. Getting tired of my hammering on this yet? If everyone has cars, then the picture is different. In this case, as long as your comparative prices are also on in-stock units, the in-stock unit may be your best bet, especially if you're closing in on a price increase.

A legitimate *incoming* unit means one that appears on the dealer's actual incoming monthly allocation. It's on some sort of list. The allocation comes over the phone initially, so don't be unnecessarily put off if your salesman shows you the back of an envelope or a scrap of paper with a bunch of manufacturer's model numbers scrawled on it. As a matter of routine the import car salesman does a tremendous amount of his business based on the allocation, and so, in his eagerness to filch a copy of it before his fellow salesman, he may have photocopied it in its rough form. In short, the list is more than likely real.

If you're shopping at a dealership with very few cars, and they show you an allocation with a bunch of lines drawn through various units and buyers' names written over them, and they also show you a price on one of the available units that is lower than what you've been quoted elsewhere, their price is also apt to be real. But you do have a judgment call to make.

Remember that games are often played. Although I actually have had cars dropped off allocations with no explanation made by the distributor, there are dealers who routinely sell their cars to the highest bidders and use this legitimate (albeit rare) occurrence as their excuse. There are dealers who will simply tell you that for whatever reason your car just didn't come in as expected. Unless you have a vehicle identification number on your order, you've no way to prove this has happened to you. Even with a vehicle identification number, to cover yourself you'd almost have to stake out the dealership and examine every incoming unit as it was taken from the transporter.

So your judgment call is this. How do you feel about the honesty of the people you're dealing with? If you think they're being straight with you, and in the vast majority of cases they will be, take it. This is one of the unavoidable risks of the game if you're going for the best possible price.

The *locate* unit is the one you need to watch the most carefully, for a number of reasons. For example, you don't have a vehicle identification number, do you? The dealer has a clear field to fill first the order that makes him the most gross profit. This leaves you still waiting for your car. If you should get mad and go somewhere else, what has the dealer lost, really? He's simply gained more profit by sidestepping you to get to a more lucrative deal.

One tactic to use on locate cars is to give the dealer a time limit in which to fill your order. I wouldn't give a dealer more than a week or two to locate a car. The car in question is either going to be out there in someone's inventory or it isn't. Why does a sales manager or his designate need more than a week or two to make a dozen phone calls to his surrounding dealers?

Whatever you do, though, don't get cute and give a locate-type order to more than one dealer. You gain nothing by doing this, and if both dealers find the car for you and then go to the expense of a dealer trade, you stand to lose your deposit at one place or the other. Often there are more than one of any given model available in the cumulative inventory of an area. Do yourself a favor and play it straight.

To put this availability-versus-price issue in its simplest terms, think of it this way. From a reliability standpoint the best unit is the in-stock unit. You know your price is real, not subject to any last-minute manufacturer's price increases. You also have the advantage of being able to drive and inspect the exact unit you're contracting to buy, which has some distinct advantages.

In terms of best price, the incoming unit is likely to have the edge. We are back to talking about the dealer who sells out of his allocation because his lower price structure has the effect of minimizing what he can keep in stock. The open-ended questions are: Will you get your car before the next round of price increases (or else there goes your price advantage)? and Will your car come off the transporter in good condition?

The locate unit is the wild card. Here you have the least amount of information and the least amount of protection. If the price is good, give it a shot, but use a realistic time limit. If the dealer won't accept the time limit, he has as much as told you what he plans on doing with your order.

How do you analyze all of the different shades of availability to price? It all depends on how much of a chance you want to take for whatever actual price difference you've managed to negotiate. At least now you have a better understanding of the risk.

THE MYTH OF PRICE PROTECTION

When you finally make a decision and order your new car from whatever dealer, the common reaction is to relax and wait for the happy phone call telling you to come and pick up your new car. Of course, now you realize a bit more about the process than the average buyer, so you probably suspect that you aren't out of the woods yet.

The fact is, your negotiations may not be quite over. For instance, suppose your new Toyota comes in with a power package (power windows, power door locks, that sort of thing) that you weren't expecting. "But," you say, "that isn't my car! I didn't order the power package! You can't expect me to pay for something I didn't order!"

"Fine, sir," your salesman says. "I can understand how you feel, but you must realize that your options at this point are to accept the car that's come in, with a slight price adjustment for the additional equipment it has, or wait a while longer for the next car to arrive."

If you're truly excited about taking delivery of your new car, how many calls are you going to get like this before you start to consider giving in? How many price increases are you going to endure before you've actually cost yourself money? Suppose you end up paying more money anyway, and without the benefit of the power package?

You're aware of the vagaries of the ordered car by now. You know that the dealer is doing little more than monitoring his incoming allocations in the hope that he can fill your order. It's understandable that if he can get you to take delivery on something that's close to what you ordered, and improve his gross profit in the process, it's worth a try for him and for his salesman. Nobody makes anything from your sale until you actually take delivery. They want your money in their bank as soon as possible. You have to understand what's going on and make the decision that meets your needs.

Of course, this sort of treatment is much more common when you're dealing with a locate-type car and when you've failed to give the dealer a time limit. You always run the risk of having a salesman who's holding two orders for the same model. If one has a higher gross profit and if he's worried about losing the deal to another dealer because of the possibility that his customers are continuing to shop, you may be waiting longer than you thought.

Chances are your salesman won't call you and tell you, "Hey, look, if you want to ever actually take delivery on the car we agreed to sell you for this ridiculously low price, you're going to have to cough up another five hundred dollars." What's more common is a string of calls offering you cars with additional equipment. This is a much more subtle way to "bump" people than the old-fashioned way of calling the customer and telling him to come on down to pick up his new car, knowing full well that when he gets to the dealership some "mistake" will be found in the deal that the customer will be asked to "take care of" or at least "split the difference" on.

The object is the same, of course, but the technique is more refined. After all, you're dealing with an import dealer, not those guys down at the domestic store. You should expect to be "mugged" with more finesse, right?

The car business is a "today" business, but the immediacy goes both ways. If you buy an incoming or locate-type car, cut the dealer's operating flexibility as much as possible. Let him know that you won't wait around indefinitely for your new car. You want to be that shaky customer they're worried about losing, not the one they think they can put off time and time again.

There is *no* price protection on an import car. It's that simple. There are just too many indirect ways to alter your agreement for you to be complacent. Realize that that colored piece of paper with all of those smudged numbers written on it is meaningless until your new car is sitting in your driveway merrily leaking oil and coolant.

THE GETAWAY

Most people are uncomfortable being impolite. Even so, a person's innate fear of salesmen, and especially of an automobile salesman, raises his emotional level to the point where he feels he has to be abrupt in order to maintain a "safe" distance from the threat of the salesman. The "I'll call you, don't call me/No, you can't have my number/The very idea of your trying to sell me a car when I told you I was just looking" routine is painfully familiar to anyone who has ever sold cars for a living, even for a short time.

Just relax and be yourself, and realize that when it comes time for you to leave the dealership, no one can stop you. They aren't going to abduct your children, chain your ankle to a desk leg when you're not looking, or let the air out of your car's tires (well, it might not hurt to keep your car parked where you can see it).

All anyone is ever going to do is ask you to buy a car. If you can say the word *no*, you've got it handled.

You will have to contend with various closing techniques. These techniques will intensify when you begin talking about price quotations, but your one reliable rampart is the simple truth: "Yes, I do want a firm price quote, but I intend to comparison-shop before I buy a car."

The market on import cars does change, sometimes quickly, because of price increases, uneven availability, and even the season of the year, but you must know by now that the profit margin a dealer will accept doesn't usually change drastically overnight. With this knowlege in mind you should be able to duck with confidence the "buy it now, or the opportunity will be lost forever" ploy, which is a staple of the automobile business.

To protect yourself and the validity of your information, you are going to do all of your price shopping over the course of a few days. Don't make a buying decision on the basis of one price quote. Comparison shopping is the only real way to find the market. Remember our magician friend? He doesn't want you to have the chance to analyze his magic, does he? His livelihood is on the line if the mystique is allowed to be stripped away.

Realize, too, that the dealer who goes to the greatest lengths to keep you from comparison shopping is usually the dealer who stands to be the least competitive when the smoke clears. The dealer who knows he is competitive will be far less threatened by your intentions. In fact, when he learns that you are an "almost today" buyer, and it's to your advantage to make your time frame clear, he'll be more than helpful.

Here's yet another axiom. Quite often the dealer who consents to give you a price quote, knowing, of course, your intention to comparison-shop, is the dealer who will produce the lowest ultimate set of numbers. Even the fellow who "lowballs" you with an absurdly low price just to get you back in his store before you buy, knows that you probably won't buy a car from him unless he's competitive. You won't come back to him, discover he's lied to you, and then proceed to buy a car from him for a higher price than you found elsewhere.

So, when it's time to leave the dealership and complete the process of collecting your price data, just follow through with what you told your salesman in the beginning. If he presses the issue, simply remind him of what you told him at first: "I always comparison-shop before I buy a car, and I'm always glad that I did." Thank him sincerely for his time and effort, and then leave.

If he becomes obnoxiously argumentative, try: "If the price you've given me is competitive, you shouldn't be concerned if I get a few prices for comparison, should you?"

By all means, make sure your salesman has your name and correct phone number so he can follow up with you later. If he doesn't know who you are, or how to contact you, when the sales manager suddenly sees his rate of sales slipping and tells his salesmen that they should call all their current prospects and offer to improve the prices by a hundred dollars or so, you won't know about it, because you were too smart to let the salesman have your phone number. Communication is the cornerstone of negotiation. Every time the salesman calls you, trying to find some way to get you back into his dealership, you'll probably make money. Don't be annoyed when the phone rings; thank the man for his call.

Getting away from the dealer can be painless, as long as you've been honest about your intentions from the beginning. On the first visit to the showroom, you tell your salesman you're interested in the product and, for the moment anyway, not the price. When you come back to that same salesman for a price a day or two later, you identify yourself as an individual who does what you say you're going to. As a result you'll come a lot closer to getting the dealer's best legitimate price quote the first time around, if for no other reason than the

salesman's subconscious wish to reward loyal customers—
they tend to be few and far between for most salesmen. When
you come back the third time, after you've done your price
gathering at however many dealerships you had the energy
for, the salesman assumes two things. One, you've learned
what the market is on the model you're after; and two, when
you impose a condition to your offer, such as a time limit on
a locate car, you're serious.

THE PYRAMID PRINCIPLE

The pyramid principle I'm talking about here has nothing
to do with those crazy marketing schemes of a few years ago.
It has to do with a certain tendency of the buying public. It
has to do with moderating or tempering your approach to
getting the best deal possible on your new car.

Imagine that the top few blocks of a pyramid are synonymous with the dealer's asking price, complete with all the
premiums and packages he's managed to think up. Some people come into a dealership and buy at that price. Perhaps
someone they trust told them you can't negotiate the price on
an import, or some other such nonsense, so they don't even
try. The fact is that these people always end up impaled on
the very top of the price structure. If you happen to be one of
these people, right now you are a very angry person.

The middle area of the pyramid represents the place
where most of us operate. I'll buy, you'll buy, most everyone
else will buy, if they get some kind of a discount that looks as
if it might be reasonable. If you made an attempt to play the
game well and the payments don't break the budget, what the
hell, right?

Then we come to the bottom row of the pyramid. These
people won't buy anything unless the person selling it to them
is losing money on it. They're fanatics. They end up buying
the car that is sold with the largest discount, not realizing that

this means they will be driving what the public has learned through experience is the least desirable product on the market. These are the people who scream the loudest when they hear their trade-in is worthless. Cars bad when new seldom improve with age. These are the people who shop for years before they buy a car, obviously believing there is some magic way to beat the realities of the system. Every car salesman has one of these individuals who routinely drives him crazy.

I doubt if this book will help those few people at the very top of the pyramid; they usually don't do much research before they buy. However, you people in the middle have already moved several steps farther down the price pyramid. You're doing just fine, as long as you don't take all of this information and overdo it. Don't become a fanatic; just become a smarter buyer.

DREAMS FOR LEASE

It's predictable that when you go car shopping, you're going to fall in love with more car than you'd planned on having to pay for, and the dealer will be right there to explain how you can "stretch" your monthly budget to float the car of your passion. One of the things he'll be pushing is auto leasing. "Why, in a few years, no one will want to own their car," he'll say. Funny, I heard that a few years ago and yet most people still prefer to buy rather than lease. What's the story? Should you buy or should you lease?

THE BASIC DIFFERENCES BETWEEN LEASING AND BUYING

The basic differences between leasing and buying a car aren't really complex. For instance, if you buy a car and finance it through a bank, you don't hold the title on the car; the bank does. If you want the title, naturally, you have to pay off the bank. Leasing is exactly the same: the bank holds the title; you have the car as long as you make your payments.

Want the title? Pay off the leasing company or bank that holds it.

So far no problems.

One of the more highly touted features of a lease is the small amount of money it takes to get involved. However, no-money-down loans are spreading across the country at a rapid rate, so even this feature isn't much different between the two financing forms.

One of the dangers of a no-money-down loan is that if you find yourself in need of a different sort of car or simply need to get out from under the payments early in the term of your agreement, your loan balance can easily be higher than the current value of your car, either in trade or on the open market. Remember upside-down Charlie? The same is true for a lease. Terminate early at your own risk.

Some of the other similarities are: you pay your own insurance, maintenance, and repairs either way you go; you also pay the full property taxes. You are totally responsible for the well-being of the car. So what is the difference?

At the end of your loan term, you own the car. At the end of the lease term, you don't. From a purely functional standpoint, this is the major difference. So why does the dealer take such delight in complicating his explanation of leasing? Because there's gold in these complications.

He knows that what you don't fully understand can be easily misrepresented. Sound familiar?

Suppose you're looking at a nice little Volvo 740 GLE, but what you'd really like to have is the 760 Turbo with the power sunroof and the full-size horses under the hood. Suppose I tell you that you can lease a 760, the car you really want, for the same money it would take to buy the 740? Suppose you're looking at a Celica versus a Celica Supra, a standard Prelude versus an SI. If it weren't for the difference in monthly payment, most people wouldn't agonize long over such a decision, would they?

This is the strongest appeal of a lease. Because of how the

amortization is structured, a lease is less costly per month by a substantial amount. What most people don't understand is how easily they can end up paying a premium on their new car, and a premium on their lease payment, without ever knowing what went wrong.

What we have to do to make you smokeproof is to take apart a lease and see how it works. Let's start with the fundamentals.

WORD GAMES

The first thing you'll discover when you start asking about leasing is that for some reason all of the terms that people conventionally use to describe such things as price, interest rate, and balance due, aren't the same anymore. So let's start with a little word game. Below, in the column on the left, you'll see our old familiar friends, the terms we understand. On the right are their "lease-speak" equivalents. See if you can match them up.

Price	Capitalization cost
Term	Term
Balloon payment	Residual
Interest rate	Money factor

Did you feel as if you had to change anything around to make the columns match up? No? That's the point. The people who thought up leasing didn't have to change anything either. *Capitalization cost*, or *"cap cost"* as it's most commonly called, is nothing more than price. Yet you will have salesmen tell you that cap cost isn't really what you're paying for the car. He'll be right, because you'll actually be paying more. *Term* is the one refreshing exception. Probably because of lack of imagination, it refers equally to lease length and to loan length. *Residual* means residual balance due, or literally *"balloon payment.*" And of course the last little gem, *money factor*, which is nothing more than interest rate.

STRUCTURE

There are four legitimate factors used in a lease computation, and a fifth that creates a problem for you quickly if you don't recognize it for what it is.

The four real factors are the price of the car (cap cost), the interest rate (money factor), the balance due at the end of the lease term (residual value), and of course the term (length of lease). All four are negotiable. The fifth factor is called "dealer reserve" or "cash flow," and for all I know, other names as well. In any event, it's a stray factor that is synonymous with "add-on," "premium," "surcharge," and so on. It's an additional figure that is superimposed on the real lease computation, and often misunderstood or completely ignored by a buyer.

Don't mistake the figure labeled "cash flow" for the amount over sticker already represented in the cap cost, or any other nonsense. This is a separate profit-making tool, a covert tactic of the first order. It's one of the reasons dealers love to lease cars. It gives them the opportunity to almost double their normal profit on the unit involved. It's why I implied earlier that the cap cost might not be what you're paying for the car, that you might in fact be paying more.

FUNCTION

How do we legitimately compute a lease then? How does this animal function? Where do all of the numbers and factors come from that tell us how much it really costs to lease a car?

Basically, a lease is nothing more than a variation in amortization. Instead of dividing the total amount of the loan into a payment structure that ends in a zero balance at the end of the time period, the lease divides the amount in such a way that there is a balance remaining at the end of the period, thus the term *residual*. It's literally a *residue* left over from incomplete amortization.

This means several things: because your payments don't have to add up to the total amount financed, they're smaller; and because your unpaid balance decreases less each month than it does in an ordinary loan, you actually pay more interest overall. (If you decide to buy your leased vehicle at the end of the lease and finance it, you *really* make the bank happy.)

Let's take a closer look at the factor termed *residual value* and see what we can learn about it.

Because the financing institution knows that it will probably get possession of the leased vehicle at lease termination, a great deal of thought and study goes into how high the residual can safely be. Most banks publish a schedule of residual values for distribution to dealers to let them know just how high they can go and still "buy the paper." Residual values usually allow for a margin somewhat under what the projected wholesale value of the unit is, and are an excellent indicator of true resale value.

This is not to say, though, that the dealer will give you the full benefit of the allowable residual value. Because of the operation of the equations involved, a higher residual means a lower monthly payment for you; a lower, more conservative residual, a higher payment. Why would this concern the dealer? Simply this: many dealers have an arrangement with the bank or banks they do their leasing business with to acquire their own lease turn-ins. What do they usually buy them for? You guessed it: the residual value stated in the contract.

To put it as plainly as possible, if you were kind enough to accept a low residual value on the car you leased, you gave the dealer the opportunity to make additional profit from his used-car operation. He'll buy your car for his used-car lot for a price he couldn't get any other way. This is another reason that dealers love to lease cars.

Now let's talk about money factors. Just as with a standard loan, the dealer often has an agreement with the bank that he may charge a customer an interest rate over and above what the bank actually requires and then pocket the difference. With a standard loan contract you can glance at the annual percentage rate, compare that to what you've been quoted elsewhere, and know immediately if you're getting a reasonable deal. Not true with a lease. In most cases you'll see a breakdown of what your payment consists of in dollars and cents: so much depreciation, so much interest or money factor, so much tax, game over.

You'll find yourself sitting there with a pencil in your hand and a blank piece of scrap paper in front of you with no idea how to equate that dollar amount to a real interest figure.

Watching the lease figured in front of you won't help either, because leases are figured most rapidly using a factor that a mathematical genius would have difficulty interpolating in his head.

The problem is the residual value again. If you have a $10,000 car with a $5,000 residual at lease termination, simply applying an interest rate to $10,000 does not tell you what your interest charges are. The residual amount is an amount that is not reduced in principal over the term. This means you're paying *interest only* on that part of the financed amount. The other amount, termed *depreciation*, is amortized more or less conventionally.

To make matters worse, the residual is not the same in every case. Whether through differences in negotiated numbers or differences in the specific models, it's possible to have any number of different residual values to factor into the equation.

What's done is this: the cap cost is added to the residual value, the sum of which is multiplied by a factor. Then the difference of the residual value and the cap cost is divided by the term of the lease, and the two elements of the payment are added together. Presto! You have your lease payment. Who can tell you the accurate interest rate involved?

Let's plug in some numbers and see what happens:

Cap cost	$10,000
Residual	$5,000
Term	48 months
Money factor	.0045*

Money factor computations:

$$\$10,000 + \$5,000 = \$15,000$$
$$\$15,000 \times .0045 = \$67.50$$

Depreciation computations:

$$\$10,000 - \$5,000 = \$5,000$$
$$\$5,000 \div 48 = \$104.17$$

Lease payment before state and local taxes:

$$\$67.50 + \$104.17 = \$171.67$$

Just for kicks, the payment to amortize a $10,000 loan fully for 48 months at approximately 10 percent interest is *$254.16*. Was that your jaw I heard dropping? Play with the amortization equation I gave you. How much more expensive a car can you lease rather than buy for the same money?

(For the sake of the nitpickers among you, yes, my number is $4.16 higher than the result the equation I've given you will produce, simply because I cheated and took the payment out of my amortization book. Remember, I told you your figures would be slightly low.)

Now do you see why so many people get excited and breeze right by the dirty details? They want to believe in magic. They suddenly see their dream car within their grasp

---

* Actually, a little over 10 percent.

and they go a little crazy. Let me bring you back down to earth.

If, instead of quoting the legitimate figure of $171.67, the dealer quoted $191.67, leasing your new car would still appear to be more than $50 a month less expensive than buying. Most people would readily think of how they could spend that extra money. They would suddenly become very happy in most circumstances.

So would the dealer. If he decides to take the full $20-a-month overage as *dealer reserve*, his profit on the lease increases by $960. That's $960 out of your pocket, and you'll never even know it. The obscene part is that you still think you're getting a good deal. In fact, you'll probably send in all of your friends for the same deal with a hearty recommendation.

Your residual value could have been underquoted, too. If, instead of the full $5,000 residual used in our computation, the dealer wrote that figure back to $4,000, the resultant change in your lease payment would be $16.93 a month, for a payment of $188.60. Of course, in this case the dealer has to wait until you turn in your car in order to benefit. Ultimately, he gains by being able to buy your lease turn-in for a $1,000 better price. You still lose $812.64 in the meantime.

The third tactic a dealer could take would be to boost your money factor. If he went to .0055 instead of .0045 (a real change of about 2 percent) that would make him (and cost you) approximately $15 a month, or $720 by the end of the 48 months.

The sad thing is, I haven't exaggerated anything for the sake of dramatic effect. The numbers involved are just this volatile, and to make matters worse, the very complexity of an auto leasing quote creates an inherent advantage for the dealer. It's all too easy to do any of the above to someone unfamiliar with leasing. You could fudge any one of the factors involved, or perhaps a combination of them, and the average leasing neophyte wouldn't know the difference. Is it any wonder both import and domestic dealers are so excited about auto leasing? Could it be any more obvious that the dealer is the last person you should ask to advise you on the question of whether you should lease or buy?

SOME THINGS YOU CAN'T DO WITH A LEASED CAR

There is no "generic" lease agreement. Everyone seems to have his own. What you might be able to do under the terms of one will not automatically be allowed under the terms of another. Some of the more common limitations imposed on a leased car, however, include the mileage limitation, restrictions on how early you may terminate your lease, where you can take your leased car, the condition in which you must maintain it, how much insurance you're required to carry on it, and whether or not you have the right to buy the leased car at any point during or after the lease term.

Mileage on a passenger car is usually restricted to 15,000 miles per year, up to a high of 18,000 miles per year. Beyond these figures you can *buy down*, or adjust, your residual figure at anywhere from six to eight cents per mile. In other words, you pay more money per month so the bank is left with a car they "own right," a car they can liquidate without losing money. Even with residual buy-downs, however, most leasing companies and banks will decline a lease when the estimated mileage will be in excess of 25,000 miles per year. No one wants to deal with a car with over 100,000 miles on it at turn-in. The leasing dealer doesn't even want it back.

If you know what your projected mileage will be over the term of the lease, the mileage limitation need not be a problem at all. You *can* get yourself in trouble with this, however. Take, for instance, a certain banker I know who was promoted to a marketing position about three months after she leased her new car. Suddenly she was driving many times the miles she had set her lease up for. Just previous to the one-year mark in her lease, she called me on the phone, told me she now had 40,000 miles on her one-year-old car, and wanted to know if she was in any trouble. I was tempted to tell her no, not as long as she drove no more than 10,000 miles, total, in the next three years, but I didn't have the heart to be flippant.

I thought bankers read everything. I thought they were the originators of fine print. Apparently I was just as wrong about bankers as most people are about car salesmen.

If she had read her particular lease, she would have known that a charge would be made of *ten cents per mile* for any mileage over the stated amount in the lease. Her 48-month lease called for a maximum of 15,000 miles per year, or a total of 60,000 miles at the end of the lease term—a very common set of parameters. If her car managed to stagger that far before it expired, she, of course, was going to have driven it 160,000 miles. In case your calculator isn't handy, this works out to a mileage penalty of $10,000.

Her only option, beside the one that involves breaking several federal and state laws, was to buy the car out of the lease early, refinance conventionally, and take her beating.

And what a beating it was going to be, because no lease builds any equity during the first year. In fact, most leases prevent a buyer from even terminating before the one-year mark. This means you buy a used car for its new-car price— mileage, dents, bald tires, and all. And don't forget, you've been making regular payments on this car as well.

So let me stress this point one more time: if you're going to lease, be sure you know *without doubt* that your projected mileage isn't going to change drastically.

Another fact to be aware of is that banks don't like to see their leased vehicles taken out of state, and certainly not out of the country. It tends to make them feel insecure. Just where are you going to drop off the car at the end of the lease? Kansas City, Missouri, or Anchorage, Alaska? They won't send the state police after you or anything, but you will definitely hear a nervous voice on the other end of the phone line when you announce what you're going to do. If you've ever looked for a way to make a banker uncomfortable, this is it.

Now that we've mentioned it, even dropping the car off at the bank can have its moments. Your lease is sure to indicate some basic guidelines pertaining to the acceptable condition of your returned vehicle. Bald tires, ripped upholstery, and unrepaired dents the size of a Yugo fender are definitely out. What almost anyone is looking for is normal condition. The tires don't have to be brand new, just well within legal limits. The upholstery doesn't have to be perfect as long as it hasn't been obviously abused, and the odd parking lot door ding most likely won't get even a mention. Naturally, the engine's emission equipment should be hooked up and operating. Just use common sense here and you've got it made.

Now we come to an interesting area, one in which you can actually pick up an advantage, provided that someone hasn't preempted you. I'm talking about the "option-to-purchase" clause that you will find in some lease agreements. It can be a winner for you if you've leased the right car.

We've already discussed the fact that the residual value is generally a conservative number as it relates to the market value of the leased car at the end of the lease term. Often it's a figure that falls below what a dealer would legitimately allow you in trade. Certainly it's a figure that could be significantly bettered on the open market. The good news is that most options are based on this number. Some, but not all, dealers will attempt to write in an option figure that is $500 to $1,000 higher than the actual residual value, in yet another attempt to maximize their lease profits. But there are a good number of dealers who haven't caught on to this latest trick.

I personally wouldn't consider leasing a car without an option to purchase clearly written into the contract, and the only option figure that would be acceptable would be the straight residual amount. An option under these terms is a fairly good "automotive future," if you will. It gives you the opportunity to recoup some of your money if the market is favorable to you, and it costs you nothing. It entails no risk. Having an option to purchase your car either during or at the end of the lease doesn't mean you *have* to; it only means you *can*.

If you still have access to the Kelly Blue Book or the NADA price guide, do a little informal research at this point. Pull out your newspaper and match up some of the better imports on an original-price-new-versus-asking-price-today basis. You'll find some of them have done extremely well. Compare the numbers in front of you in the book. Look at the wholesale figures with the realization that your option price should be something less. The conclusion you'll ultimately come to is that there are some cars out there that are better for you to lease than others, considering the option you might be able to get. And you'll realize that you can buy the right car out of a lease and then sell it privately for a several thousand dollars' profit. Would that excite you? If it *really* excites you, have you thought about a career in the car business?

CROSSING SWORDS WITH THE INDEPENDENT LEASING AGENT

If you're serious about leasing a new car, there's an animal out there in the automotive jungle that acts a lot like a dealer, but he doesn't have a franchise, or a service department, or a parts department, or three hundred cars in stock. In fact, he doesn't sell just one or two makes of cars, but the whole spectrum. He's the independent leasing agent and sometime automobile broker.

He's also someone you should talk to before you make your final decision about leasing.

Don't get me wrong, he knows all the same maneuvers

the dealer does, plus some. He's by no means a tame lion. But he does have something to offer. Even though he may add his profit structure to what he actually had to pay the dealer for the car he's leasing to you, he just might save you money.

How's that?

Let me explain it this way. If you spent the good part of your day, sometimes seven days a week, buying cars from dealers to fill your leasing customers' orders, would you know where the deals are? If you've managed to stay in business very long, you'd have to.

Now, here are a few of the hard facts of life for the independent leasing agent that will make his situation clear.

People come to leasing agents in the first place because they're shoppers. They've already been to the dealers and now what they're after is a better deal. If all the independent leasing agent ever did was call his nearby dealers, pay the going rate, and then attempt to pass his own additional markup on to his customers, how many cars would he deliver? Would he ever deliver *any* cars? The gullible customers go straight to the dealers. The independent has to bring down the smart buyer nearly every time. What kind of hocus-pocus is going on here?

I'll tell you. Because of the differing economic climates in different regions, the market price of any given import car also differs; sometimes dramatically. When I moved from Southern California to the Midwest, I was shocked to find out that, on the exact same make of car I'd been selling, the average gross profit in the Chicago area was *half* of what it had been in the Los Angeles area. Not long after I began selling imports in Connecticut, I learned that the dealers in nearby Vermont were selling some models for as much as $3,000 less than my dealership was routinely getting. Obviously, then, the door is open for an enterprising independent who's not afraid to run up his long-distance phone bill a little and then pay a few drivers to shuffle some cars around when need be.

This is the main reason independents can stay in business, and even prosper. But there are a few more you should know about.

If you do a certain number of leases with some banks, you can arrange a special discount lease rate. Usually, the number of leases needed to qualify for such a program is high, to encourage both loyalty and production. However, when an independent leasing agent does manage to get in the program, he suddenly has an edge. Remember our games with money factors on page 57 and how a small change in money factor increased the lease payment by $15? A little break here and there on his buy rate can make a substantial difference to the independent. It can keep him in the game, even when he's having trouble locating cars he can place with a customer for a conventional profit.

Which brings us to the next point. Independent leasing agents don't have the same overhead as the dealers. They aren't paying thousands of dollars in floor plan every month to maintain a hundred or so new cars on a sales lot. They don't have several acres of prime commercial real estate hanging around their financial statement. No big light bill. No big tax bill. No fifty employees. Independents, as a rule, aren't afraid to take a small piece of the pie if that's all they can manage. Show an independent how he can make $300 or $400 on a deal, and then by all means don't stand in his way. Kind of a refreshing attitude, isn't it?

But don't be lulled into a false sense of complacency. If you don't shop, if you don't know what a good deal is, you open the door for these individuals to do rude things to your financial statement, and they'll do just that. Count on it.

There are also a couple of other things to consider. The independent leasing agent seldom deals with a regular salesman. Instead, he deals with a "fleet/leasing manager" at the dealership. At some dealerships this special manager sells far more cars each month than the best of the regulars. He works a forty-hour week, usually has weekends off, almost never works nights. To the salesman on the floor he seems to have the softest job in the dealership, in addition to the fact that he is constantly raiding the inventory and making it difficult for the salesman to meet his sales quota. To put it in plain language, the fleet/leasing manager is almost universally hated in the dealership. The fact that the owner and general manager have put him on a drastically reduced commission schedule, in order to maintain their targets for gross profit per unit, is always overlooked. This man has a monopoly, true enough, but he does pay a price for it.

Part of the price he pays, and this involves you as well as your independent leasing agent, is that if the sales manager can select which unit goes to the leasing customer, it's always going to be the shabby one. The one with scratches, or some demo miles, or some other niggling problem. You are a second-class customer in the eyes of everyone. Since they didn't get your money, they don't care about you. If you have a problem, so what, you should have bought the car from a regular dealer.

On a more positive note, keep one thing in mind: the full factory warranty still applies, and the manufacturer and his distributor are just as interested in your happiness with their product, even if the dealer didn't get the chance to hang you by your big toes.

AN OPEN-ENDED PROBLEM, A CLOSED ISSUE

If you started off this chapter with a fair understanding of leasing, one thing that's probably surprised you is that I haven't talked about the differences between the two most common forms of leases, namely the open-end lease and the closed-end lease. I haven't because no one ever remembers for very long which is supposed to be which anyway, and I want you to read your individual lease agreement in full.

As I've stated before, there is no generic lease form. All

leases contain their own little surprises, and as a result deserve to be read until understood.

Understand just one feature that differentiates the two forms of leases and you will know as much as you need to know to select the closed-end lease over the open-end lease.

Remember our residual value? Remember the dissertation on how careful the bank is to set it within certain conservative limits? This is because in a closed-end lease the figure the bank places on the turn-in is preset in the very beginning. Beyond obvious mileage and condition considerations, it is a closed subject. It just doesn't matter to the buyer if the bottom drops out of the market for that particular car. If he brings it back in decent shape, he walks.

The value of the car at the end of the lease term is more of a problem in an open-end lease. The mechanics of the procedure vary from lease to lease, but generally some attempt is made at the close of an open-end lease to appraise the car to establish the operative residual value. Quite simply, a buyer can be responsible to a significant extent for a change in the market value of his turn-in. I don't know about you, but the only time I like to be surprised is on my birthday.

In fairness, the advantage of an open-end lease is that a lease company can be more speculative with the residual value. They can eliminate more of the safety margin inherent in the figure and as a result lower the lease payment. And why not? If they guess wrong, you're going to pay for their mistake.

DEATH, TAXES, AND NOW LEASING

Because of the recent changes in our tax laws, leasing is destined to become a much more prevalent form of auto financing. In a few years the auto loan interest deduction will be completely phased out, thereby eliminating one of the larger advantages of buying over leasing. Investment tax credits are completely gone, again eliminating an advantage that was much more accessible and clear-cut to a buyer than a lessor. And, of course, prices keep increasing each year, making the lower payment structures of leasing ever more necessary and attractive to the regular new-car buyer. In short, it's much more likely you'll be involved with an auto lease now than ever before.

This means that, for a while anyway, a fortune in windfall profits will fall into the dealers' laps. You've already seen just how they'll do it. I hope it spurs you into learning this material backward and forward so you can protect yourself. I hope you go to the trouble to call the bank direct and get their residual formula on the car you're interested in so you can spot-check your salesman. (And if they don't know what you're talking about, keep calling until you reach someone who does.) I hope you shop the money factors in the same way. And by all means I hope you spot any stray factors such as dealer's reserve or cash flow on your payment breakdown. And please remember this: comparison shopping applies with equal force whether you're buying or leasing.

I'm really not trying to talk you out of leasing your next new car. Just recognize how many new pitfalls there are to learn about and prepare yourself well enough so you don't wind up being anyone's "highest gross profit of the month."

▪ 5

BONES ABOUT LOANS

So, let's say, in spite of all of the so-called marvelous benefits of leasing, you've decided that you'd rather buy than lease your new car. And there's no problem there because the dealer can handle the financing on a straight purchase, right?

He certainly can, but there are some things you should be aware of before you let him, the first of which is the fact that a dealer usually does only what he thinks will, directly or indirectly, make him money, or at least give him more control over his customers. Realize that there are no Swedish Ford Motor Credits, no Japanese GMACs, no German Chrysler Credit Corporations, and that there must be, for the import dealer, an in-house, direct profit motive in providing financing on new and used cars.

BEHOLD, THE MIDDLEMAN

The bank (and I use the term *bank* to describe a catchall of various lending institutions, including savings and loans, thrift institutions, credit unions, and the like) is the primary source for your loan funds. You should never forget this simple fact. The dealer is not your lender. He's an agent of the lender at most, and he functions as such in order to make money and gain control of his customers.

Typically, a dealer will attempt to charge a customer from ½ percent to perhaps 2 percent over the bank's minimum acceptable interest rate. On a $10,000 loan with a 48-month term this amounts to some money, approximately $200 over the life of the loan for each whole percentage point of increase. On the same $10,000 loan, but with a 60-month term, the figure becomes closer to $250 per whole percentage point.

In fairness, the dealer does perform a service to earn this money. He usually prepares your loan application and all loan papers right at the dealership, saving you some running around in the process. Often he allows you to purchase your new car for a smaller down payment than you might ordinarily be able to arrange, because he may retain some responsibility for dealing with your repossession if you should default. Thus, by no means is the dealer's interest rate overage an entirely surplus charge. It's only a problem when it's abused or when it becomes excessive. Your protection is to pick up the phone and check the prevailing loan rates. If you don't take this simple step, you can be certain your oversight will cost you money.

Regardless of the validity of the dealer's charge for arranging your loan, however, and regardless of the convenience it might afford you, I recommend strongly that you arrange your own financing. And my reason has nothing at all to do with saving $100 or $200 on your total finance charges.

HE WHO CONTROLS THE LOAN CONTROLS THE DEAL

The average automobile salesman, whether import or domestic, hears this little slogan every time he turns around.

It's a topic of conversation at the vast majority of his sales meetings. Finance and Insurance (F&I) penetration, meaning the ratio of buyers who dealer finance compared to the ones who finance outside, is closely monitored. You can be certain the salesman gets a stern talking to if he runs into a streak of customers who decide to shop their own loans.

Now, the dealer isn't really all that concerned about a couple of hundred dollars extra profit on each of his units. By the time he pays his office help to do the loan documents, and by the time he pays commissions on the overage, he isn't actually left with much. No, the loan is just one cog in the works of a larger mechanism, a mechanism that can generate as much or more profit than the sale of the car itself.

THE ART AND SCIENCE OF COVERT NEGOTIATION

We touched on this earlier, and I promised you an explanation in greater detail. No doubt you remember our discussion on how dangerous it is to rely on the salesman to quote accurate payments. Realize that it is a matter of policy at most dealerships to intentionally quote payments that are high by some dictated margin or another. Some dealers will tell their salesmen to factor in an additional $500, some as much as $1,000 over and above the actual loan amount. Some will have the salesmen automatically include life, accident, and health insurance; some, the additional amount necessary to buy an extended warranty. There are practically as many variations on the theme as there are individual dealerships. The only given in the equation is that the payments quoted by your salesman will likely be higher than the actual figure.

Bad enough, but often the salesman doesn't stop at simply quoting you a higher payment. If you allow the dealer to arrange your financing, and if he manages to structure a time lapse between your buying visit and your interview with the F&I manager, he'll quite likely take your freshly filled out credit application and have your loan preapproved for the inflated amount as well. Furthermore, if the additional amount causes your loan application to be declined, he'll keep trying different banks until he gets "his" amount approved. Suddenly your credit report can start to look like a Who's Who in the banking community. On paper you'll look like someone who's having a great deal of trouble placing his auto loan. Not a happy situation in the mystical realm of loan committees and loan officers.

Did you give him permission to test your credit limits? Not exactly, certainly not intentionally. But if you signed the loan application, you gave him written authorization to check your credit. It's all part of how a dealer gains more information about you, to help him sell you additional items beyond the car itself. And information along with preconditioning are extremely powerful tools.

Now assume you're sitting in front of the F&I manager. Not only does he know that you've been preconditioned to an artificially high payment, but he knows exactly what he can sell you and still get your loan accepted at the bank. Two trump cards instead of the one you've already learned about.

Suppose you've been preconditioned for just $25 a month over the actual payment? Not an outrageous amount, not an amount the majority of people would detect, certainly, but if you remember the practical amortization equation (see p. 20) you know that $25 equates to $1,000. That's a fair amount of operating room for most F&I people to have. You had to fight hard to get a discount on your car; now the dealer stands to gain back all of the ground he lost and then some.

But if you don't consent to buy anything additional, they have to draw up the contracts with the actual numbers, don't they? Yes, of course, but the subtleties of contracts escape most people who aren't trained attorneys, and remember you're looking for a higher payment than you're apt to see in the appropriate block on the contract.

Q: That payment is less than I was expecting. Is it accurate?
A: Yes, sir. Including your loan insurance and everything, it's accurate according to the computer. That is the interest rate you were quoted, isn't it?

Do you see what happened? I made a sandwich.

Do you like pickles? My little girl doesn't, but when she accidentally gets one in a hamburger, sometimes she swallows it before she realizes it's there. Even if she still has half of it in her mouth, she's reluctant to spit it out because it's embarrassing. Most civilized people would do the same.

In my example above, the low payment, which you are sure to notice, is the top piece of bread. The interest rate, which you are specifically asked to check, is the bottom piece of bread. The pickle hidden inside is, of course, the life, accident, and health insurance you don't really notice you're swallowing. (You don't notice the $15-to-$20-a-month charge for insurance because your payment is a few dollars less than what you were conditioned for. If you'd been quoted the proper payment, it would have been obvious.)

It's all written down on the contract, right there for you or anyone else to read. The law even requires a minimum size of print. However, lots of people don't bother to look for the "pickles." Lots of smart, normally careful people allow themselves to be distracted. Even the ones who go home, sit down with the paperwork, and study it (no doubt after they've shown the neighbors their new car and bragged about the deal they got) are generally too embarrassed to get up and go hash it out with the dealer. It's easier to figure they've been had and let it go at that.

Do you doubt that this happens quite often? Go back and look at some of your own old contracts, if you dare.

Not all F&I people make a practice of sneaking in the back door. Some—the less successful ones—enjoy the sport and challenge of trying to sell products marked up 300 and 400 percent. They smile a lot, tell clever stories, the whole bit, but even if they choose to play the game a bit more aboveboard, they still have their trump cards. They still have the psychological advantage of knowing that you're expecting a higher payment than is legitimately required. They will do their best to keep some of that money, one way or another.

My last dealership added one more wrinkle to the game plan. The buyers were never allowed to see the F&I manager until their loans were set. This was a hard-and-fast rule. The salesman processed the loan with the bank and then handed over his customer to the F&I office when everything was in order, meaning that the buyer's now artificially inflated loan amount had been fully approved.

In this case, of course, the finance manager had been relieved of the job of placing the loans and could concentrate on adding high-profit items to the deal after the sale. Instead of being called the finance manager in this configuration he was dubbed the delivery coordinator, a brand-new veil to hide behind. You saw him ostensibly to schedule your delivery for a convenient time. If you happened to be pitched on extended warranties, rustproofing, pin-striping, sunroofs, and security systems at the same time, so what?

Did this little ploy work? Yes, surprisingly well. It seems that many of the people marched right in, excited about their new car, refreshed, receptive, and with their guards down because they weren't expecting to have to do battle with yet another salesman.

Watch for this new procedure. It works so well it's bound to spread.

THE PERILS OF *SPOT* DELIVERY

Spot delivery is nothing more than immediate delivery. When you agree to buy a car, you fill out a credit application, hand over the down payment, sign off your trade-in, put your name on about twenty-five other innocuous-looking documents, and they deliver the car to you "on the spot." It's the preferred way to do business in some areas of the country, though quite rare in others. Whatever the situation in your particular area, the spot-delivery method has more pitfalls than a video game, and you should be aware of at least a few of them just in case you ever have to contend with the system.

A dealer who chooses to use spot delivery must do a great many things differently from the more traditional dealer, who usually has a few days to deliver. For instance, he has to have an individual in his employ who is capable of reading and understanding a credit application, as well as a credit report, and can reliably determine if a car can be financed for this buyer. It logically falls to the F&I manager to make these determinations; however, not all F&I people have the same batting average.

Even with an accurate credit application, a clearly read-able credit report, and a good idea of the bank's underwriting requirements, the dealer still finds himself in the very shaky position of second-guessing another professional, namely the bank's loan officer. When you add the questionable skill of the F&I manager as a variable to the problem, you can see how mistakes can be made. If a customer misstates his income, or the amount of his rent, or the amount of cash he has in savings, then, understandably, the percentage of unfinance-able deals inadvertently delivered can go even higher.

Why would a dealer choose to run his business in such a dangerous manner? *Profits.* As they're driving home in their new car, very few buyers stop off at the next dealer to see how good a deal they really got. If they paid $1,000 over market, they don't know about it, because their comparison shopping has just been preempted. Suddenly, they're in a hurry to park that new car in their driveway and start attracting the gaping neighbors.

It's a great ploy. Even though these people haven't actu-ally bought this car, because they aren't yet financed, they certainly *think* they have. The dealer has their down payment, their trade-in, their signature on everything, not to mention a stack of their empty Styrofoam coffee cups. These people have someone else's car parked in their driveway, and if they don't qualify with the bank, for whatever reason, that car will disappear.

It's amazing how quickly people can come up with a co-signer when the alternative is losing the new car they've been driving around in and bragging about for the last two days.

It's amazing how quickly they overcome the embarrassment of having to ask friends and relatives for money when the bank tells them they have to make a larger down payment in order to get their loan.

It's *astonishing* how quickly they'll agree to pay a higher interest rate than the one originally agreed on when they're told over the phone that the only lender that will touch them is a thrift and loan in Tijuana that needs another 2 percent in order to make the loan.

You might think a dealer takes a tremendous risk by spot-delivering a new car under uncertain circumstances, but the truth is he often has more cooperative buyers to work with because of it. The greatest risk is taken by the buyer, which is just what the dealer prefers.

Buyers don't intend to let their loan arrangements get out of their control. They think the dealer knows what he's doing. The percentage rate is clearly marked on the contract, so are the payments, the down payment. On the surface it appears that all of the details have been taken care of.

However, in the heat of negotiation, the buyer tends to forget that the dealer isn't the bank, that he is only an agent for the bank and is not empowered to make any final decisions pertaining to loan approval. Look at the contract you just signed. Did anyone from the bank sign it before you left the dealership?

Suppose, instead of letting the dealer arrange your loan, you decide to do it yourself. First, you go out and find the car you want to buy. Because you believe you need a purchase order before the bank can process your loan, and because you want to know what your loan amount and payments will be, you negotiate price. It's a difficult negotiation, and you feel you have a good deal. You offer the dealer a deposit to hold the car until you can arrange your loan. So far so good. Unless you failed to comparison-shop, you haven't made a mistake.

The dealer says fine to all of this, but with one condition. You write a check for the down payment, you sign a "one-pay" agreement, and you accept delivery of the car today. He tells you you've made him cut such a small deal he doesn't want to hold the car and continue paying floor plan on it for a week to ten days while you shop your loan and get it approved. An understandable point to most reasonable people.

A *one-pay* agreement, however, is a full-fledged financing contract. It in fact spells out terms and conditions that will apply to you if you are unable to place your financing else-where within the time limits specified. Seldom is the interest rate stated the best possible one, but because you won't be financing with the dealership anyway, you'll probably ignore it. However, unless someone in the finance office or the sales staff makes a mistake, before you leave the dealership they will have every piece of documentation they need to process a loan without your having to return to the dealership. What all of this means is: make one false step and you're going to stumble right into a loan that you don't want.

I know of a case where the buyer signed a one-pay agree-ment and was unable to arrange his own financing. In fact, his credit was so bad that the dealer couldn't get him financed either—don't ask me why they delivered the car in the first place. The final twist was that the dealer had sold the buyer's trade-in in the meantime to a wholesaler who immediately bought tires, some other mechanical bits and pieces, and paid for a complete detail job (cleaning and polishing). The whole-saler was in the process of taking the car to the local auction when he was called by the dealer and asked to return the car because the deal had been rescinded, or "unwound."

The wholesaler, who had operated from the beginning in good faith, simply wanted to be reimbursed for his reconditioning work. If it hadn't been for his attitude in the matter, the buyer would still be in lawsuits today.

If you take spot delivery utilizing a one-pay agreement, at least seek preapproval at your bank. Even though your salesman may tell you otherwise, the bank doesn't need a specific purchase order to tell you how large a loan they will approve you for. And by all means know what their processing time is. If you take longer to get your loan than your agreement allows, then you're in trouble.

THE ALL-NEW AND IMPROVED METHOD OF DISCOUNTING

For the past several years domestic manufacturers have been offering extremely low interest rates on new-car loans to generate floor traffic and, of course, sales. It's been working very well; so well, in fact, that the import dealers have countered the tactic with some low-interest-rate promotions of their own. Notice I said import dealer, not manufacturer.

The result of all this financing wizardry has been the establishment of a brand-new method of discounting cars and what has turned out to be a very effective way to confuse the comparison shopper. How do you compare a price discount to an interest rate discount? How much is a 4.9 percent loan worth in comparison to a 6.9 percent loan?

Let me explain some of the hard realities of banking. Banks lend money to make money. If they're paying you 7 percent on your money-market account and they lend out your money to a car buyer at 2.9 percent, when the stockholders find out, someone is going to get fired.

It's obvious that something is going on behind the scenes.

Someone has to be paying the bank to make these otherwise foolish loans.

Let's take a look at the basic mathematics involved. Remember when we were talking about how the dealer marks up his percentages on the loans that he arranges? We used a $10,000 loan with a 48-month term and said that each whole percentage point would equal about $200 over the course of the loan. Suppose instead of marking up the banks' percentages, the dealer chose to mark them down? What would it cost him? About $200 per each whole percentage point? That's right, as long as we're talking about a $10,000 loan based on 48 months.

If you examine the fine print in any of the low-interest-rate ads, though, you'll make a discovery. The dealer will have put limits on both loan amount and term offered. This is what he's trying to do: the same $10,000 loan, but based on 24 months instead of 48, will cost him only $150 per whole percentage point decrease; a $5,000 loan based on 36 months will cost him approximately $75 per each whole percentage point decrease.

Let's say that the current *buy rate*, or dealer's wholesale cost of loan money, at the bank is 10 percent. You as a dealer want to offer 2.9 percent for a weekend sale to generate a little floor traffic. You offer a $5,000 loan at 2.9 percent for 36 months on any cars you have in stock. The cost to you per loan? Let's see, you're buying down the interest rate 7 percent. Seven times $75 equals $525.

Now answer this question. Doesn't it seem as if a 2.9 percent loan should save you more than just $525? Now you understand why dealers love this little game. You also realize why, if you examine the ad in question, the lower the interest rate offered, the shorter the term of the loan and the lower the loan amount allowed. This is simply how the dealer is limiting the amount of his discount.

Here's an idea for you. If you shop your own interest rates, independent of the dealer, you might just catch a bank in the process of doing a little marketing of their own. Often banks will lend money at a lower rate than normal to generate new customers. Some are even brazen enough to call what they're doing a "loan sale." The point I'm making is this: Why not take advantage of the bank's marketing *as well as* the dealer's marketing? Wouldn't you rather give yourself a chance at discounts in both areas instead of just one?

While you're at the bank, ask your loan officer to tell you what, based on the parameters in the ad, the difference would be between the finance charges of his loan versus the dealer's loan. In other words, have him establish the approximate cost of the dealer's buy-down. Be sure you compare same to same in all respects. This figure should automatically give you a clue to what kinds of minimum discounts are available from the dealer of the car in question. With this information in hand, under no circumstances would you accept a discount offered by the dealer at a lesser figure. (Is this a little covert negotiation of your own? Heaven forbid!)

With the new tax laws eliminating the interest-rate deduction, it is clear that the low-interest-rate method of discounting is going to be with us indefinitely. Unfortunately for the buyer, it means that he will have to keep track of even more factors than he had to previously if he expects to negotiate effectively. It's become more important than ever to do some preparation, get outside information, and then take a systematic approach to establishing the true market value of the car you want to buy.

CAN THE PROMOTIONAL INTEREST RATE ACTUALLY BE A BETTER DEAL?

Let's not overlook one possibility. For all of your figuring and estimating, you really don't know what each dealer's actual buy-down rate is at the bank. He certainly won't tell you. There is the outside possibility that when you compare total cost to total cost the specific low-interest-rate deal you're looking at will have an edge. If it does, there's nothing wrong with going for it. It's all just money. As absurd as it may seem to you, it is now possible to pay more for your new car but, because of the financing package, have a better deal overall.

So, how do you call it? Simple. Add the whole thing up and compare bottom lines. Go right past the total of purchase price, tax, and license. Add these items to the finance charge and look at what you have. (If you don't have the total finance charge available at your particular stage of negotiations, have the salesman compute it for you, and then double-check to see that it remains the same on your actual contract. Don't be any more afraid to ask for this information than you would be for the price.) This is the new bottom line you're going to use from now on. It's always been the real bottom line anyway; we've just never trained ourselves to look at it.

6

USED BUT NOT ABUSED

Not too long after I began to sell cars for a living, I ran into a customer with a unique slant on the question of whether to buy a new or a used car. When I approached this rather well-dressed individual and asked him how I could help him, he was emphatic that I show him only used cars. He wouldn't even consider a new car, no matter how good a deal I implied he might make. When I asked him why, he gave me an answer I've never forgotten.

"I'll tell you something, my boy. A new car is the only car you can buy and be absolutely certain that every nut, bolt, and wire on it has been recently tampered with. I'd rather have a car that's had some field testing."

Warranties aside (even though you can buy extended warranties on most used cars anyway), the man had a point. Over years of watching the service lanes and after a brief stint as a service manager, I learned that new cars indeed do break down with regularity. It's just extremely difficult to put over two thousand parts together, right, the first time.

So, perhaps before you rush out and plunge into a brand-new set of high-tech wheels, you should give some serious consideration to a car with a little experience, or as my man said, "some field testing." Who knows, you might just save some money in the process.

SOME WEIRD GROUND RULES FOR BUYING
A USED CAR

At the opposite ends of the spectrum, there appear two archetypes in used-car buyers, and in between them about 200 million variations on the theme.

One of these individuals would never dream of buying a used car from anyone other than a private party, whereas the other seems to seek out the dealer at all costs. The one who does it on his own has a handle on his finances, and more often than not he's a cash buyer. Predictably, the dealer-only fellow always needs some help in this area. The first gentleman steadfastly believes the dealer's reconditioning efforts consist of changing the sawdust in the differential, wiping the grease off the old spark plugs, and spinning the odometer back fifty thousand miles. The second gentleman naïvely expects that the dealer has returned all his used cars to the factory for comprehensive reconditioning. Only rarely do either of these individuals modify their thinking, even when faced with hard evidence that there are exceptions to every rule and some advantages to be had in the broad area between their two positions.

Quite frankly, the nearer you are to either of these two extremes the less good this chapter and this section will do you. What I'm going to do is talk to the middle. I'm going to tell you to consider buying a used car from a dealer, an individual, or perhaps still another, unexplored alternative.

Let's be flexible in our thinking. Some of the approaches I put forward are admittedly untraditional, but they do work, so they're worth talking about.

NEVER GO TO AN XYZ DEALER TO BUY A USED XYZ

I've seen this happen many times. A dealer will take in a different manufacturer's clean but expensive car as a trade-in. The car will be practically ready to park out on the front line just the way the customer dropped it off. The entire sales force will begin to salivate over the huge gross profit they imagine this unit will command. Then, to everyone's amazement, a wholesaler arrives, sometimes within minutes, to drive the unit away. Why?

Simply this: a Mercedes buyer doesn't make a habit of shopping for a clean used Mercedes on an Isuzu dealer's lot, and any given dealer knows it. Worse than this, even models that you would imagine to be close in concept and therefore should logically share a common buyer pool, such as Toyota and Honda, or Audi and BMW, tend not to cross over automatically. The typical Volvo buyer routinely goes to the Volvo dealer when he wants to find a used Volvo. The same goes for a Subaru, a Nissan, and other makes. The only way dealers sell "foreign cars" (literally, foreign to *them*) is by either force of advertising or happy accident; a buyer just happens to see the car in question on the dealers' front line. Very few people come looking for a specific used car at a dealership they know specializes in a make other than the one they are interested in. And even if a dealer does manage to lure that stray buyer, he has still another hurdle to clear before he can capitalize on the situation: his own salesmen.

The reason for this is that many import dealers allow their new-car salesmen to sell both new and used cars. Naturally, members of any given sales force will be more familiar with their own product than that of their competitor, so they'll be less skilled when faced with having to sell something "different."

As an example, a Honda dealer is better equipped to sell a Honda than anything else. Not only does he ordinarily have more prospects for his own cars, but his salesmen are more effective in dealing with them. And let's not overlook the fact that he'll also be able to handle any warranty repairs that occur after the sale with less trouble and fewer headaches because of the specialized expertise of his service department.

From your standpoint, however, a Honda is a Honda, a BMW a BMW, no matter where it is. Why would you want to pay top dollar for your used car simply because of where it happens to be parked? Or to put it another way, if you could save $500 to $1,000, or more, why not walk across the street?

And this is just what can happen. If you are a Volvo buyer and you see a Volvo on a Toyota dealer's lot, immediately you have an advantage you wouldn't have at the Volvo dealership. Even more so if you're a buyer for a Mercedes, Audi, BMW, Jaguar, Porsche, TVR, Lotus, Alfa Romeo, or any other specialty car you can think of. As a rule, any kind of a specialty car generates an unwelcome flood of people into a dealership who yearn for an opportunity to engage in mindless "car talk." Dealers and their salesmen would much rather sell cars than talk about them. A hot exotic or specialty car usually drives them crazy until it's gone. Your interest might be one of the few opportunities for the dealer to put a quick end to all the nonsense, plus help him avoid a straight nonprofit wholesale turnover. Once he knows you're actually serious he'll like you, and you'll have a good shot at saving some money.

SERVICE IS A DIFFERENT STORY

Let's stop and touch on something that isn't universally realized. It isn't smart to take your "different" car back to the dealer for service just because you bought it there. He more than likely isn't as well qualified to perform its routine service as your car's "home" dealership. The more complex cars have become, the more specialized the mechanics—they're called "technicians" now—have become. The days when a tune-up could be done with a handful of greasy tools and a feeler gauge have been gone for a long time. The days when a mechanic was simply a mechanic and was qualified to work on any car are just as certainly over.

To underscore this fact, when I was promoted out of the sales department to be a service manager, I was surprised at the amount of specialized "service-bulletin"-type information that was accumulated on a routine basis from the manufacturer. It was immediately obvious to me that a service department, no matter how good, just isn't going to have the same advantages and support when it steps into another manufacturer's product, an observation that quickly bore itself out many times over.

What usually happens is this. There are two categories of technician at any given dealership: the flat-rate technician who is paid according to the number of jobs performed, and the hourly mechanic who is paid for the duration of his work. It's difficult to coerce a highly qualified flat-rate technician to work on an "oddball" used car to begin with, unless there's no other work to be done, which is seldom the case in a busy dealership. The flat-rate man is understandably more enthusiastic about doing what's familiar and therefore quicker and more profitable for him.

So your used car's service work will probably be dispatched to either a junior flat-rate technician or an hourly mechanic; in either case, a man who hasn't developed his skill to the highest levels and who certainly won't know every nuance of the complex systems in your vehicle. It's an inescapable fact that as comprehensive as any dealership's library of repair manuals might be, it won't offer the same help as the manufacturer's accumulation of service bulletins and point-specific "inside" information.

None of this should be a surprise to you, but as unlikely as it sounds, a substantial percentage of used-car buyers persist in returning to well-meaning but unqualified service departments for their service work, simply because they purchased their car at that dealership.

INTO THE LION'S CAGE FOR FUN AND PROFIT

There are just a few reasons why a dealer would pass up the opportunity to make a substantial retail profit on a trade-in and instead sell that unit to a wholesaler, or directly to another dealer, for what amounts to a zero profit. All of these reasons, of course, relate to how quickly and how easily he can make a sale on a particular unit and to what his prospects are for making and keeping a profit from the entire venture.

Some cars taken in trade are hopeless, but not all wholesaled units are beat-up, high-mileage derelicts that are beyond usefulness. As I've indicated earlier in this chapter, some trade-ins are wholesaled simply because they aren't a make or in a price range that the dealer feels he can effectively market.

What this means to you is that a good many perfectly sound used cars are bought and sold on a market just below the surface of the dealer level. It's a huge secondary automotive market in which cars change hands at prices, in some cases, *thousands of dollars below* the levels of the current retail market.

Many people play this market. Some of the major operators move hundreds of thousands of dollars in and out each month with the ease and sophistication of a Wall Street stockbroker. It is by no means safe ground for the uninitiated. But the market exists, and a private buyer can gain entrance to it more easily than you might think.

Realize that what I am about to describe to you is fraught with risks. I want you to understand this in the clearest possible terms. There are more ways than you can imagine to end up with a terrible car and absolutely no recourse. You'll be going in blind and unprotected, fresh bait in a sea of sharks. But if you have a strong sense of adventure and if the idea of buying a car so cheaply that you can drive it for a year or two and still sell it for a profit appeals to you, then by all means let me show you how you can enter the realm of the wholesale auto auction.

Theoretically, it is forbidden for a private individual to attend a wholesale auction as a buyer, but many do just this, albeit in the company of a bona fide wholesaler. Your first task will be to find just such a wholesaler who is willing to cover for you, but first I shall disclose a few of the hard facts of buying a car at auction.

If you can't make a quick decision, don't waste your time with this approach. Needless to say, you won't be given an opportunity to go home and "think it over." Auctions run on the excitement of the moment. Big winners and big losers happen at a rapid pace.

If you don't have ready cash to consummate your purchase, few wholesalers will bother with you. They'll probably just invite you to visit their retail lot during regular business hours.

If you have to have one specific model, one particular color, and only one model-year car, count on its being at the auction either the week before you attend or the week following. In other words, don't bother.

You must be willing to do a little advance research on the wholesale book values of a few different cars ahead of time. No wholesaler is going to spend his time nursemaiding you into the right car at the right price. Remember that the only reason he might consent to take you to the auction is that you will pay him a fee for the privilege and you won't interfere with his operating time. You're his "easy" money, not his mission in life.

One thing you might find helpful to study is the summary of the results of the previous few weeks' auctions. In one way or another, all the various auctions supply this information to the dealer community as a service to help them appraise their trade-ins. These auction sheets, or auction reports, provide a "today" look at the current used-car market that is more accurate to a particular region, and, of course, much more current than either the latest issue of the Kelly Blue Book (which comes out only every two months) or the NADA guide. The auction sheet alone will indicate to you whether there is enough of a savings to be had on the type of car you are interested in to make it worthwhile to attend. Ask your friendly wholesaler for these sheets; he's sure to have a desk drawer full of them. And realize that there will most likely be other private buyers lurking around who in their excitement may bid the value of the car in question beyond what would be a good deal for you. You have to know when to stop bidding, period.

Now, how do you find this wholesaler in the first place, and what should you pay him?

Any legitimate dealer can go to the wholesale auto auction and transact business, as long as he is in good standing with the auction. The most productive dealers to canvass are probably the smaller ones who sell older, moderately priced used cars. Many repair shops in some parts of the country also have a used-car dealer's license. What you'll have to do is make the rounds and ask the question. But, fair warning: be prepared to get thrown out of a few places before you find the right individual. Some dealers will take great offense at what you'll be trying to do, which, of course, is circumvent an entire level of profit taking, the one that affects their livelihood. I promise you, though, if you persevere you'll run across someone who will be happy to talk to you.

As far as what you should expect to have to pay, some wholesalers will ask you for a flat fee for taking you to the auction, whether or not you buy a car. Others will ask a percentage of the purchase price for their trouble and perhaps an additional amount for doing the paperwork that the law requires. I know of no set figures or percentages that are widespread. This is borderline black market we're talking about here. Whatever your particular wholesaler proposes may be totally original. My best advice is, if it sounds unreasonable to you, don't do it.

Also, not that wholesalers as a group are any more dishonest than any other businessmen, but common sense dictates that you should have a clear understanding of what is going to happen from the beginning to the end of the process and that that understanding should be written down and signed by all parties. You should have a breakdown of all fees. You should know who will be doing the registration work on the car and how you will be expected to handle payment. Make an attempt to clarify just who is to do what, and when, before you commit your funds. (You may not be able to get the wholesaler you find to agree to put all of this in writing, but I want to be on record with the recommendation.)

For every major wholesaler there are probably a hundred small-time operators just scraping by. Many of them are small-used-car-lot operators who in a good month might sell half a dozen units in retail and trade another dozen at the local auction. Some have no lot of their own but work under the umbrella of a new-car dealership or a friend who does have a small lot. The arrangements that these privateers concoct are as numerous and varied as the law allows, and sometimes beyond, but one thread is common: virtually all of them are looking for whatever profit they can make, whatever way they can make it. To protect yourself, you have to proceed on the assumption that if you give them an opening they will take your money.

Have I frightened you sufficiently to keep you away from the auction? If so, there's another tactic, almost as dangerous, but much more accessible. Read on.

WHY YOU MIGHT WANT TO BUY AN "ODDBALL" CAR ON PURPOSE

A few years ago there was a huge amount of publicity about the lawsuit Ford was involved in over the contention that the fuel tanks on the Pinto were overly prone to exploding upon a rear impact. The result of all this was that almost overnight the resale value on these cars fell drastically. For a while you couldn't give one of them away. Even after an aggressive factory recall of all the specific units in question, the resale value remained low. At this point, the Pinto became an extraordinary value on the used-car market.

French cars, for some reason, have never done well in the American market. A Peugeot, for instance, has many of the same features as a Mercedes, BMW, or Volvo, but the Peugeot's resale value, especially for diesel models, has never enjoyed the same strength. Another French car, the Renault, suffers from the same malady, even though Renault's American-built models are about as generically designed as you can get.

Another example of an "oddball" is the front-wheel-drive Ford Fiesta, a feisty little performer, still out there in numbers, even though it hasn't been imported since 1980. This car is near the bottom rung in resale value.

How about an Isuzu diesel P'UP mini-truck? A tremendous amount of transportation and utility for a minuscule price, as long as you're in no particular hurry, because these vehicles are anything but quick. (The trick here is to invest in a nice radio so you have something to do on the long ride.)

You can extend this list a good deal further with nothing more sophisticated than the classifieds from your local newspaper, a Kelly Blue Book, or a NADA price guide. The used-car buyer too often overlooks the alternatives to the popular import; generally, he turns up his nose at the offbeat cars as a reflex instead of after careful thought. I contend that he routinely costs himself money when he does this.

OK, I know that everyone who's ever read the *Consumer Reports* list of recommended used cars just gave me a zero credibility rating. But did you know that every manufacturer currently building and selling cars in this country has quite a few—indeed, thousands—of satisfied customers? Furthermore, they all have thousands of repeat customers.

The various systems for rating cars are not a matter of black and white, but rather one of shades of gray. For instance, if a car gets a reputation for a poor automatic transmission, or any other component, this is based on a percentage of failure. Seldom is such a problem across-the-board. Usually a much higher percentage of cars performs properly than not. Design defects do regularly find their way into the market; I won't argue this point. Yet there are also recalls in which the manufacturers attempt to solve the particular problem, and more often than not they do.

Depending on which magazine you read, there is only one import car of the year, but the rest of the also-rans still burn their share of the gasoline in spite of this. Take a look at the cars parked in front of the supermarket. I'll bet you see quite a few that have absolutely horrible ratings, but they're there just the same. They're doing the job for someone. Unless a car is hooked to a tow truck you know it actually runs. It's something to think about.

Cars enjoy good resale value for a reason. I'm not denying that some of the cars I've mentioned will be inherently more difficult to find parts for, or that they may prove to be less reliable overall than one of the mainstream Japanese-built cars, for example. They may not be as contemporary in their styling as they should be. What I am saying is that if I had to choose between a Toyota Celica with 90,000 miles and a Renault Encore with 35,000 miles for the same price, I'd buy the Encore. The Toyota is a remarkably well rated car but, unfortunately, every car has a limited life expectancy.

WHY *MILEAGE* CAN BE A VERY RELATIVE TERM

In spite of the example above, it's important to realize that mileage is only an indication of a car's condition. Although we live in a throwaway society, there are people who maintain their cars with the expectation of keeping them for a long period of time. Engines don't automatically explode when they reach 100,000 miles. Paint doesn't automatically curl up and flake off when a car is five years old. Even rust isn't inevitable if problems are taken care of early enough. *Mileage is relative to maintenance.*

Here's something to think about for a moment. Do you realize that the average trucker puts several hundred thousand miles on his tractor over the course of its lifetime? And tractor-trailer rigs operate under tremendous stresses and loads. Follow one up a long hill sometime and count the downshifts that are made before the crest is reached. These units work hard; yet, more often than not, they deliver incredibly good service.

Now, I'm not suggesting that your new Yugo will keep running indefinitely if you only squirt a little oil on it once in a while. Products of any type are engineered for a certain amount of use, and certainly within manufacturing cost constraints. What I'm saying is that abuse and lack of maintenance mean more than total accumulated mileage.

You can kill a Volvo in 30,000 miles if you put your mind to it. The very same Volvo in different hands might run 300,000 miles with little more than normal maintenance. I've seen high-mileage Toyotas, Mercedeses, Volkswagens, Saabs, even the odd General Motors diesel, that run fine. By no means is this a complete list. Many different types of cars, with maintenance, will operate long after the 100,000-mile mark is reached.

But no dealer will take a high-mileage car in trade for very much money. As ludicrous as it might be, condition is meaningless if the odometer reads too high a number.

What does this mean to you? It means there is a segment of the market out there where a careful buyer can buy a perfectly good car at an absolutely bargain basement price. And it's funny, you can operate in this area with practically no depreciation, because there is little difference between the value of a car with 150,000 miles and one with 180,000 miles.

Consider this. I once had a customer who was a salesman with a large territory. This gentleman drove, on average, 50,000 miles a year. He had a standing request that I was to call him anytime a nice car came in with high mileage. He knew, from some very expensive experiences, that any new car he bought would be absolutely worthless in trade in no more than a year or two, and he was tired of taking thousands of dollars in depreciation every time he traded cars.

The net result of his strategy was that he owned some interesting cars and seldom lost much money on any of them. His trick, if you can call it that, was never to buy a car that wasn't in good cosmetic condition. He figured that if it was well taken care of on the outside, then the assumption could be made that the owner did at least fundamental maintenance on the running gear.

To whet your appetite a little more, realize that a car with over 100,000 miles is generally appraised by a dealer at no more than half of its ordinary book value, less reconditioning costs, of course.

And now we come to another category of high-mileage cars that deserve a special look: the specialty cars.

No one ever takes a Porsche to the junkyard. I've seen almost total rust buckets painstakingly restored, rebuilt, and then sold for incredible amounts of money. Emotion, myth, and the total disengagement of logic are the norm with the Porschephile. Here, condition, though still not everything, definitely carries more weight than mileage. You may indeed find an absolutely beautiful Porsche to play with that happens to have several hundred thousand miles on it. Don't worry about it; just look at all the receipts to document the maintenance and at least note how expensive the parts for these cars are before you buy one.

The people who love BMWs are almost as committed as

the Porsche crowd. Many of these individuals are absolute fanatics when it comes to taking care of their cars. Again, look at the maintenance receipts, and if the overall condition is good you probably won't get burned.

I could go on. I could tell you about the couple who traded in their Volvo station wagon with 303,000 miles on it. That car still drove decently. I could tell you about the man and woman from Bishop, California, who decided to keep their 1972 Volvo for a while longer even though it had 275,000 hard miles. But what would be the point?

The fact is, no manufacturer makes a car that, given careful maintenance and reasonable treatment, won't drive well into the high-mileage zone. If you can find one of these and document its maintenance, you've probably bought yourself a good car as well as cheap transportation.

THE ACTUAL COST PER MILE OF OWNING A CAR

Let's forget about gas mileage, and insurance costs, and even the cost of maintenance. If you like to own a certain kind of car, you're stuck with whatever these factors turn out to be anyway. I've yet to see a Nissan 300ZX traded in solely because a Volkswagen diesel gets much better fuel economy. Usually there are numerous other factors involved: for example, new baby coming, can't make the payments, too many tickets. Let's forget these factors and look at the largest of all of the areas where people lose money on cars: depreciation.

The average new car generally loses about 50 percent of its value over the first four years. Some do better than this, but most don't. This means that if you buy a $20,000 car, chances are that four years later the dealer will be talking about a $10,000 trade-in value, if you're lucky. Some cars drop this much in the first year.

Average mileage for the nonprofessional is between 12,000 and 15,000 per year. That means your $20,000 new car will cost you between seventeen and twenty-one cents per mile for depreciation alone. By comparison, chances are your fuel cost was only five cents per mile (based on twenty miles per gallon and $1.00 per gallon of fuel). This makes depreciation the monster expense.

Here's the kicker. The next buyer of your four-year-old car, if he suffers the same rate of depreciation in the next four years, will have half of the depreciation you did. His cost per mile will be under ten cents (or even less, because used cars tend to moderate in depreciation the older they get).

You already knew that new cars were more expensive than used cars, didn't you? But not *this* much more expensive.

7

TRADES IN THE TRADE

Whether you decide to buy a new or used car, there's one element we haven't mentioned at all thus far. I'm talking, of course, about the used car you probably own now. What should you do with it? Trade it in to the thieving dealer, just so he can make a lot of money on it after he gives you next to nothing for it? You're expecting me to say no, aren't you?

For some reason, the rumor persists that the dealer can somehow transform that rat's nest of yours with 290,000 miles on it into a lifetime opportunity for himself. But he can't. In fact, many import dealers don't even want your trade. "But they take trades all the time," you say. "All dealers have used cars on their lots. What about that old saw that a dealer makes more money from his used cars than he does from his new cars?"

You're right back out there on the thin ice again. Let me show you why.

THE AUTOMOTIVE "BLACK HOLE"

How would you like to invest $358,000, in cash, to make $700?

No, you say? Well, you may be amused to know that my last dealer often did just this. This very smart man allowed himself to sink a ton of money into a used-car inventory in a dealership that traditionally had trouble selling used cars in any numbers to speak of. Why? The fact is a used-car inventory can get out of hand in a hurry, no matter who you are.

If lawyers visit their mistakes in prisons, and doctors bury theirs in cemeteries, then sales managers must certainly park their mistakes on used-car lots. Even the most conscientious of sales managers will attempt to bury the occasional "bone." The hitch is, it doesn't take many of these "bones" to create a problem.

Thus, the origins of the dreaded automotive *black hole*: an accumulation of used-car inventory that just won't go away; a cash-consuming monster that defies control once it reaches critical proportions. This is one of the major reasons both domestic and import dealerships go out of business, and an area where the wrong manager can literally sell his dealer's principal into bankruptcy.

To understand why this sometimes happens, even to the most vigilant of dealers, is to understand a great deal about the mechanics of trading cars in.

ACV

An ACV may sound like something you ride through the woods, but it isn't. What it is is the root problem a manager faces when he attempts to put a value on your trade-in. ACV stands for *actual cash value* as it applies to a used car.

Suppose we took that $358,000 used-car inventory and hauled it all down to the local wholesale auto auction. Whatever we could liquidate that inventory for—on the spot, in ready cash—would be its ACV. No punches pulled. No one would care if you just spent $850 rebuilding an automatic transmission; that's your tough luck. No one would care if you just had to repossess one of the units and pay the bank's loan off even though the car wasn't worth that amount. You're supposed to have the title to any car you sell at auction; it's a requirement. In fact, the amount of money you may have spent on any individual car is totally irrelevant. The only number that counts is the one that stops the bidding.

These are the hard facts. Any given used car is worth only so much in real money, no matter what the dealer might have put the car on the books for, no matter how much the sales manager might have fudged to make the deal so he could get his bonus money. The auction always determines the actual numbers.

Something should be apparent to you by now. You should be asking yourself the following question: If the auction establishes the actual value of my trade-in, does that mean my trade-in is worth the same amount of money at any given dealership I visit?

Answer: yes, plus or minus something for dealer miscalculation. You may have a bad air-conditioning compressor, but the sales manager who appraises your car might miss it. You might need a complete brake job, yet the brakes might feel fine to him as he drives your car once around the block. Sales managers aren't master mechanics; they only *think* they are.

So the sales manager (assuming he's charged with the responsibility) runs your car through the auction and it brings a bid within $600 of what he figured the ACV should be. What next? Sell it for the loss and *write the deal back* (that is, adjust the gross profit on the sale)? This will infuriate everyone, including the general manager, the owner, and the salesman involved. Or should he park it on the used-car lot and attempt to retail his way out of it?

Right; used-car lot, here we come.

Of course, now the sales manager is buried in this car to the tune of the $600 he overbid it. He can't afford to do a full-fledged reconditioning job on this little jewel of his, so the rough paint on the hood will have to stay that way. The car will receive only a minor tune-up, even though the idle isn't quite right. The stains on the upholstery will be left there unless the buyer complains and wants to make a shampoo job part of the deal.

Voilà, as they say in show business. What he has is an instant bone, properly buried on the dealer's premises, no matter that the several thousand dollars the trade may represent is buried with it.

And, of course, it's an unattractive bone, too. The car neither looks as sharp as it could nor runs as well. Understandably, salesmen don't have much enthusiasm showing shabby cars to buyers; there's too much of a chance their credibility will be destroyed before they even get started. And the salesman involved in the original deal doesn't attempt to come to the dealer's rescue, either. It isn't his problem if the sales manager blows an appraisal. The result? The bone stays buried for a while, and the problem only becomes worse.

So, what's the answer for the manager? How does he strike a balance that both maintains a healthy rate of sale and keeps his gross profits accumulating in the bank instead of on the used-car lot?

THE CONSERVATIVE APPROACH
TO USED-CAR APPRAISAL

A good many sales managers never go to an auction. They rely on a roving band of entrepreneurs—wholesalers—to liquidate the trade-ins not deemed suitable for the dealer's own used-car operation. In this case the wholesaler becomes a buffer between the dealer and the auction.

Now, why would a dealer want to insert a whole new level of profit taking between himself and the buyers at the auction? Wouldn't you think this would only narrow the dealer's own profits? Wouldn't you think he might make himself less competitive with his auction-going competition? Any reasonable person would think so, I grant you, but let's take a closer look at the function and operation of the happy wholesaler.

The wholesaler doesn't sit at a dealership and fight with retail customers all day as does the sales manager. He circulates from dealer to dealer, talking, listening, buying, and occasionally selling cars. He goes to several auctions regularly, not just one. He might even go outside of his area to entirely different markets. He couldn't care less how much gross profit a Nissan dealer should hold on a new 200SX; he cares intensely what last year's 200SX brings on the current wholesale market. He knows which auction tends to bring the best price for specific cars. He knows which auctions are infiltrated with retail buyers working with wholesalers. He's a specialist and he uses car telephones, computers, and other such devices to give him a continual feel for the market. The average sales manager is a neophyte by comparison, and he has neither the time nor the freedom to be anything different.

So where does this put you, the retail buyer with a car to trade? If you have a garden-variety used car, one that is well represented in the "book" and the auction sheets, one that the sales manager has likely seen and turned several times in the last several weeks, then chances are the sales manager will appraise your car fairly accurately on his own, without having to call anyone. The wholesaler will have educated him about how much he will be willing to pay for it, usually how much less than the current book value.

This means that a sales manager is conditioned to adjust the appraisal on your car downward to allow the wholesaler some room. It may be only a couple of hundred dollars, but it will be there consistently. You won't get the true "auction-generated" ACV for your trade. But, if the car you are trading in is the least little bit unusual, then the picture changes.

Let's say you're trading in a specialty car, an Alfa Romeo, for instance. Unless you're trading an Alfa for an Alfa, the dealer in question will be at an immediate loss as to what a "safe" ACV might be on your car. There just aren't that many of these cars on the market. In six years, I've only seen two Alfas actually traded in.

So the wholesaler gets a call, and the wholesaler gets to take a chance. If he knows the car and he knows where he can sell it, he may make a winner out of it. If he calls it wrong, he has to chalk it up to the cost of doing business, realizing that he will have to take a few "losers" to keep the loyalty and cooperation of the sales manager he's working with. You benefit from this procedure because it tends to win you a stronger bid. I guarantee that if the dealer is flying on his own you're going to get much less.

Now, here's the complication for you. By now you know how the dealer establishes a value on your car: book value or auction sheet value, less reconditioning, and most likely less an adjustment for the wholesaler. But you still don't know the number. You still don't know what your trade-in is worth.

And nobody's going to tell you.

THE GREAT MYSTERY

Most dealers can't bring themselves to tell a customer that the car he bought three years ago, possibly at the very same dealership, is now worth less than half of what he paid for it. Cars may not have been as expensive three years ago as they are now, but they were plenty expensive, and this kind of a shock can ruin the buyer's attitude quickly.

Thus, dealers fog the issue as best they can. Instead of showing you a $900 discount and $4,500 for your car, they show you a $400 discount and $5,000 for your car. It's the same $5,400 either way you add it up, but the latter looks better than the former.

Of course, the next dealer may offer you a $300 discount and $5,100 for your car, and the third dealer may have a $600 higher asking price, offer you a pitiful $200 discount, but allow $5,800 for your trade! (This last guy's *really* after your business.)

The examples above are oversimplified because we've ignored packages completely, in-stock versus incoming and locate-type cars, and all financing factors entirely. But the example does serve one useful purpose: it's an exercise in comparing discounts to trade-in allowances in the only manner that makes sense: added together and adjusted for any price differences.

You still don't have the faintest idea what your car is actually worth, though, and you need to know this number if you hope to get a clear picture of your alternatives.

STRAIGHT FROM THE STONE AGE

Every "how to negotiate with the dealer" type of book or magazine article you've ever read has suggested that you leave your trade-in out of the deal until the last minute. Then, after you've negotiated your best deal, whammo! You drop the sucker on them.

Remember our talk about the "market" on any particular import car and about how the sales manager knows what price his car should bring? Playing games with your trade-in isn't going to change his knowledge of its worth, either. He's going to make his profit on the sale no matter what.

If the sales manager does get up out of his comfortable chair and appraise your last-minute trade-in, he's certainly not going to cut you any breaks. He's absolutely not going to overlook anything in the cosmetic or mechanical condition of your vehicle.

The appraisal you see won't be the actual ACV on your car, either. In most instances it will be lower, so the manager has some room to negotiate with you further. If you tricked him once, he'll figure you'll do it again. Can you blame him?

At this point I hope you see why you'll be a lot better off

if you leave this last-minute-trade-in routine in the Stone Age where it belongs.

ASK FOR THE BAD NEWS UP FRONT

The one thing that's difficult for a dealer to avoid gracefully is the direct question, but simply asking him to tell you what ACV he's putting on your car won't do the job for you. He isn't going to want to offend you with the truth at the risk of losing you as a customer. You'll have to sharpshoot a little. You'll have to aim your question in such a way that you avoid his natural defenses.

Ask your salesman if it would be all right to see the most current auction sheets pertaining to your particular kind of car. Ask him the minute you start talking about the price of the new car. Tell him that you simply want to make a quick evaluation of whether or not you should trade in your present car or perhaps sell it privately. It's a direct question that is extremely difficult to dodge, and in most cases it will get you what you want: a reasonable idea about ACV.

If you have a fairly common type of car, examples similar to it will probably appear on the sheets, especially if you have several weeks of these to go through. Mileage and equipment are usually noted, so you should be able to draw valid comparisons. Disregard any sales figures that seem high in order to establish a wholesale ACV; remember that retail buyers sometimes invade the auction. With a little study, you should get the picture.

Now that you've seen the shocking number, what next?

SHOULD YOU SELL IT YOURSELF?

You're probably angry. There's no way you can trade in your car for a number as low as the one the auction sheets indicate it is worth!

Remember, however, that the wholesale ACV is not the total amount your trade-in is ultimately worth. If you have the time and the inclination, you can probably get more on the open market, but, as always, there are a number of factors to consider.

Time is money in the automobile business, as much or more so than in any other business. The longer you hold on to your trade-in, the less it will be worth. The longer you wait to purchase your new car, the more likely the price will increase or an availability problem will arise. You could also break something on the car, or run into something with it, or get caught in a hailstorm.

The ideal situation is to be in a position where you don't need the equity from your present car in order to purchase the new one. This way you can clean the old wagon up, stick it safely in the garage, and advertise it to your heart's content. The right buyer for it will ultimately stumble in and give you his money.

Even if you're still making payments on your old car, if you could sell it for $1,000 over its ACV, how many months would you be able to hold on to it before it sells and still make a profit? As I said, time is money, happily in more ways than one.

But the used-car business is a gambler's business, and you'd better be able to run the risk.

Unfortunately, most of us can't take a few thousand dollars out of our operating capital and still be comfortable. I've seen hundreds of credit applications, and most of the people applying didn't have large amounts of reserve cash. This is why the dealer can expect people to buy from him at retail and sell to him at wholesale, which is essentially what happens when you trade in your car. He knows that most people can't afford to inventory their used car until it sells.

If you're one of the lucky few who can, here are some tips on how to give yourself the best odds.

If it's broken, fix it. Even something as simple as a missing window crank can cost you a sale, or at the very least a good deal of perceived value in the mind of your buyer. But use common sense. If your car isn't a particularly expensive unit and it needs a new transmission or a new engine, be careful not to spend more than you can logically expect to get back. Salvage yards quite often will buy broken cars for more than the dealer's ACV. Try there before you make a large investment in repairs.

If it's dirty, clean it. It's amazing how much better a clean car looks to a buyer. If he knows he doesn't have to go straight home and put on his waders and rubber gloves, he'll come a lot closer to making you an offer. Little touches such as carefully spray-painting the wheels so they don't look quite so rusty will brighten up the car's appearance appreciably. A cheap set of floormats from your local discount store, or a little silicon spray on the dash, can also help. We're not talking big money here. How about that junk in the glove box and trunk? You'll have to clean them out eventually, anyway, so you might as well do it before you try to sell the car.

If it smells, deodorize it. Some cars you sit in can make your eyes water. No one wants a car that smells bad. If in doubt, buy an air freshener.

If it has any paint left on it, polish it. Clean, shiny paint work gives the illusion of good maintenance, besides the obvious fact that it makes the car look more attractive. Car dealers have used this trick for years. It can mean hundreds of dollars in your pocket. Even dents look better when they're shiny.

If it looks nice, park it where it can be seen. Want to go blind before your time? Read the classified ads in search of a used car. Many times people buy cars simply because they like the way they look. Parking your car at a gas station, in your front yard, or at a shopping center simply gives it more exposure. Pardon me while I state the obvious—wherever you park the thing, be sure and get permission. The money for one towing bill will buy an incredible amount of advertising.

Don't finance for anyone. Don't laugh; you may get asked. If you had bad credit, and you needed a car, what would you do?

Don't let anyone go for a demo ride alone. You may get a call from Albuquerque, New Mexico, saying thanks for the use of your car and telling you where you can pick it up. That is, if you're lucky. Remember that you don't have dealer's insurance. Repeat this tip out loud one hundred times if you have a performance car to sell.

Don't let the registration lapse. People don't buy used cars they can't drive—not for very much money, anyway.

Take cash or a cashier's check only.

Be sure to inform the DMV and your insurance company when the car is sold. Unless you want to pay someone else's parking tickets, this is important. Most states include the appropriate form in their registration package. Use DMV-supplied forms only. They're generally simple and easy to understand, plus they keep you from leaving out anything either you or the buyer may need to transfer the ownership of your vehicle properly.

Before you attempt to sell your used car, find out about any consumer protection laws in your state that might bear on your responsibilities. Just call the DMV, tell them what you want to know, and have them clue you in.

WHAT IF YOUR CAR DOESN'T SELL?

It can happen. That's why selling a car on your own is always a gamble. Yet there is a way out of the situation.

Just because you didn't wholesale your car to the dealer at the time you bought your new car doesn't mean you are locked out of the wholesale market. In fact, even if you know you're going to trade, you may want to consider the advantages of wholesaling your car yourself. You may make out better than you would at the dealer. Let's take a look at one way truly to get "market" for your trade any time you choose.

Remember our happy wholesaler, the one we talked about earlier whom you could pay to sneak you into the auction? Well, here's the news: they buy *and* sell cars at the auction, and you can play the game either way. If you want to circumvent the dealer altogether, you can. You might just snag a masquerading retail buyer who will pay you a semiretail price for your car.

Again, fees and arrangements are as varied as the individuals involved, but by no means should you simply give the wholesaler the signed-off title to your car and then send him to the auction on his own. You might just run into a wholesaler who was about to leave town anyway. In any event, you'll want to verify what your car brought in person. You'll feel better about it later.

To forewarn you a bit, there are usually several different *lines* (literally, lines of cars, motors running, waiting to move past a particular auctioneer and his gathering of buyers) at an auction. If there are four or five lines, there will be four or five separate auctions going at once, each with a different set of parameters. For instance, there will be an as-is line where cars are sold with absolutely no warranty. These cars can have doctored motors, no smog equipment, or other problems. There is generally no arbitration to speak of on these units. They also bring the lowest prices.

There will be other lines with newer cars and/or trucks that may involve disclosure of defects at the risk of arbitration. This means if a car has frame damage and you don't tell anyone, the winning bidder can decline your car or renegotiate the price. In other words, when the gavel drops the game doesn't stop.

In fairness, sometimes when the arbitrator thinks the buyer's complaint is groundless, which is fairly often, he can and will enforce the sale in the seller's favor. However, it's always better not to try to sneak anything by that's too ridiculous. Keep in mind that your buyer will be a professional. Make sure you are fully aware of any after-the-sale responsibilities particular to the specific auction you'll be going to. Discuss this thoroughly with your wholesaler.

If you've started to form a basic picture of the auction, by now you must imagine that there will be a tremendous amount of hoopla, noise, and excitement, not to mention brain-killing clouds of carbon dioxide from all those running motors. To make matters worse, even after your wholesaler's fee, the auction's fee, and all the nervous upheaval you'll go through, you still have no guarantee that your car will bring an acceptable bid. But take heart; there is one more way you can get rid of your old car, without the nausea and the splitting headache, and for a price most likely higher than the dealer's ACV. You can shop it direct.

WHO BUYS ALL THOSE CARS AT THE AUCTION ANYWAY?

Most auction cars are sold to the independent used-car lot; the small dealer who doesn't have a new-car franchise from which to build his inventory. Wait a minute, you say, are you telling me that the import dealer has huge problems making money on his used-car operation, yet other independent dealers go looking for used-car inventory on purpose?

Yes, I am. Much to the new-car dealers' chagrin, there are people out there who know how to make a dollar on a used car. They buy their cars outright, so they buy the cars that are right for their lot. They usually don't try to sell a car for as much gross profit as the new-car dealer might, which tends to keep their inventory moving. And to balance things out, they generally don't have the huge overhead the new-car dealer does. Selling used cars successfully is as much an art form as a business discipline, but the artists are out there.

If you make the rounds with these people, and if you

have a car that is fairly decent, you might be surprised at how well you do in comparison to the numbers the auction sheets might indicate. Realize that when you sell direct you eliminate the wholesaler's profit margin. There are real possibilities here, so don't neglect them. You might be infinitely better off taking on one pro at a time instead of three acres of them at once.

TRADES, APPRAISALS, AND THE ORDERED CAR

There's one possibility we haven't discussed. What happens to your trade-in allowance if it takes a few weeks or perhaps a few months for your ordered car to appear at the dealership? We talked about some of the perils of the locate-type car, but we didn't clarify this point.

Your car isn't going to stop depreciating in value just because you and the dealer signed a retail order. He knows it and you know it. This means the trade-in he's going to get from you will be worth less and less the longer he takes to produce and deliver your new car; hence, the gross profit on his sale to you will be smaller.

No harm done if your car shows up in ten days. But what about ten weeks? In ten weeks your car could have been devalued twice in the Kelly Blue Book—which comes out every two months in an updated edition. Other popular price guides have similar publication spans. The bottom line is that your car could be worth several hundred dollars less on the wholesale market by the time you hand over the keys, and no dealer is going to expose himself to this possibility if he's in his right mind. This is why, on the back of your contract somewhere, you are sure to find a clause that limits the time frame for which your appraisal is valid. Usually it's no more than thirty days; often it's fourteen.

Does your house have a front door and a back door? Most contracts do, as well. One thing virtually all retail contracts spell out is that you have no protection against a legitimate manufacturer's price increase. That's the front door. What I'm pointing out now is that if you look, you'll find you have no protection against a reappraisal of your trade-in if delivery of your new car is delayed beyond the stated time frame. This means that if your dealer chooses to wait a bit before he finds your ordered car, he's in control of the negotiations again. This is the back door to the contract.

The price guide won't help you. The auction sheets won't help you. The contract won't tie your appraisal to either one of these in any way. What you'll be faced with is the whim of the dealer at the time of his reappraisal.

Want the car? You'll pay more money. Want to take your trade-in out of the deal at the last minute to dodge the problem? "I'm sorry, sir," someone will say, "but the trade was part of the deal. If you take it out now, you've voided your agreement, and we start all over." Suddenly, both price and trade-in value are open issues again.

See why I don't recommend locate-type orders without a time limit—maximum time limit—recommended? Right; read the time frame the dealer wants on your trade-in value. *You* take control. If you don't, the dealer will be happy to.

WHY YOUR NEIGHBOR, AFTER THE FACT, WILL ALWAYS TELL YOU HE WOULD HAVE GIVEN YOU MORE FOR YOUR TRADE-IN THAN THE DEALER

Some things happen with such regularity that they have no entertainment value whatsoever. One of these things is the statement your neighbor will make when he finds out what you got in trade for your old car.

"Gosh, John, I would have given you five hundred dollars more than that for your old car, if you'd given me the chance," he'll say.

Want to have some fun of your own? Grab his hand

vigorously and tell him, "Gee, that's great, Harry! I thought you might be interested in the old car, so I made the dealer agree to give me the option to buy my car back for the next ten days. We sure could use the extra five hundred dollars!"

The longer you stand there and pump his hand with a big smile on your face, the more your troublesome neighbor will sweat and the more creative his excuses will become for not buying your old car. How far you push it depends on how mean you are. The point is, if he really wanted to buy your old car, he would have let you know before now.

A GAME THAT BANKERS LOVE TO PLAY

Right in the same vein as your neighbor's annoying little game is the one your banker likes to dabble in.

He has a wholesale price guide, remember. The minute you tell him what the dealer has offered you on your old car, he'll crack open his book, frown pensively, and say something like, "Well, in my professional opinion they should have given you another fourteen hundred dollars for your car, but I guess what's done is done."

Start discussing the auction sheets from the last couple of sales, ask him which auction he prefers to attend. Drop some terms such as *ACV*, the *arbitrator*, the *as-is* line. See how fast you find yourself talking about the stock market.

▪ 8

NEGOTIATION:
THE RULES OF THE GAME

By now you know what to expect from the import dealer. You should know what kind of transaction meets your needs, what kind of car you're after, what buy or lease payments you can handle, and that your loan should be preapproved before you set foot in the dealership. Now, and only now, are we ready to discuss the actual "negotiation" process, the greasy nuts and bolts themselves.

Finally, here's some good news for you: good buyer negotiating skills aren't active so much as they're passive. The professional across the desk from you will be the one on the offensive. All you need to cultivate are some good defensive skills. The buyers who were the most successful with me worked defensively, and I've listened to the same thing happen, over and over again, to my fellow salesmen.

We're going to start by listing a few rules that you must recognize before you begin. Cumulatively, as a salesman, these little gems cost me a lot of money, so pay attention.

RULE NUMBER 1: WHEN OVER YOUR HEAD, CONCENTRATE ON THE FUNDAMENTALS

Mild confusion is a salesman's best friend. Not the kind of confusion that keeps someone from making a commitment, just the kind of uncertainty that tends to convince a buyer to listen to his salesman. He'll ask you questions that challenge your ideas on what you can afford to spend and how soon you will be ready to make a final decision. Some of these questions and their answers will be dead logical. Some will zero in purely on your emotions. If you keep your mind centered on the most basic aspects of your task, however, it will be very difficult for any salesman to snare you before you've done enough comparison shopping to enable you to make a properly informed decision.

What kind of monthly payments can you afford? What kind of car meets your needs? Have you seen enough different kinds of cars to satisfy your curiosity? Do you have enough price data from enough dealerships to know what the market is on the car you want? Don't buy until you've filled in all the blanks.

Be polite, but don't be afraid to be stubborn in your goals. When necessary, remind your salesmen of what your goals are for each particular visit to the dealership. Keep coming back to them each time you're challenged. These are excellent defensive weapons. Employ them.

RULE NUMBER 2: RECOGNIZE THE FACT THAT YOU ARE THE ONE WHO BENEFITS MOST FROM NEGOTIATION

"I don't understand why you dealers have to play these stupid games. Why can't you just give me your best price and stop wasting my time?"

Are you guilty of saying something along these lines? If so, I want to call you aside and have a little talk.

The dealer has a price on his car. It's in black and white. He'll let you pay that price without a single game being played. You won't have to be bothered with negotiating at all. Now, doesn't that make you happy? No? Then you'd better pull your head out of whatever dark place it's in at the moment and open your eyes.

When you negotiate, which way does the dealer's price go, up or down? Who benefits? Certainly not the dealer; when you negotiate, he loses money. You must realize that if you're to get any kind of a reasonable deal on your new car, you're going to have to play the game, at least to some extent.

You can't change the game. You can't change the rules. Either develop some basic skills or stay out of the ballpark. Otherwise, you'll only make a fool out of yourself. Something like 25 million new and used cars were sold in this country last year. Billions of dollars changed hands in a certain way. Do you really expect to stop this mega-industry in its tracks, just because you don't want to "stoop" to do a little negotiating on your $6,000 Mitsubishi?

If I've made you angry with this little dissertation, good. You of all people have the most to gain from what I'm attempting to do here.

Chances are you've never been comfortable trying to negotiate because you haven't known how. That's what this book is meant to assist you with. Keep in mind that I'm not telling you to do anything that isn't perfectly honorable. I've told you that lying to the dealer will only backfire on you. Time and time again I've told you that it's the right information, the truth about the market value of the car you want, that will make the difference for you.

Negotiation isn't a dirty word; *ignorance* is.

RULE NUMBER 3: DON'T FIGHT THE DEALER'S "SYSTEM"—RECOGNIZE IT FOR WHAT IT IS AND WORK WITH IT

Dealers work with a lot of people, sales staff as well as customers. To reduce the level of confusion and increase efficiency, they've had to develop certain set methods of operation. Because of the various methods in use, one dealer may do things a good deal differently from another. Your salesman may have to follow certain guidelines for him to proceed with your requests. There may be seemingly silly inflexibility on certain issues. The best approach is to go in with an open mind, follow the procedures, if at all reasonable, and stick to your game plan. Bucking the system only complicates the issue.

If you do business with a very small dealership, the salesman might be responsible for negotiating your entire transaction. You might even be sitting across the desk from the owner himself. More than likely, however, there will be several levels of players that separate you from the actual decision maker. Don't be annoyed if you feel like a cow in a herd. Try to identify the authority level of the person you are dealing with at the moment and save yourself the trouble of leaving the dealership with meaningless price or trade-in-value information.

Most books about the car business you've ever read talked about the dreaded "T.O. house" and the high-pressure tactics it employs to "beat people up" until they consent to buy a car. The fact is, the *T.O. house*, or turnover house, where you are passed from salesman to salesman before they give up on you, does usually produce higher gross profits and a higher percentage of sales from the gross numbers of customers through the door. Such dealerships play on the "fatigue factor" to do it for them. You keep seeing one bright, fresh, friendly face after another until you either get tired and sign on the dotted line or throw your hands over your head and go screaming and flailing out the door.

It's true, some dealers feel that before they let a customer walk off the lot a second salesman should be given a shot at making the sale. And a different approach, or a different personality, sometimes does make a tremendous difference. The second salesman might be a "closer," a special "almost manager" type who is adept at eliminating certain kinds of reservations in a buyer's mind, or he might be just another ordinary salesman. Don't be overly concerned; no one can keep you from leaving the dealership when you are ready. When you have what you need, just get up and go—and don't forget, even these people will usually sell a car for its market value, whether today, tomorrow, or next week. You get the idea.

The other end of the spectrum is the *straight-sell house*, in which the salesman either has no manager at all to confer with or perhaps has just one. You'll feel more like a human with a dealer who uses this method, but it doesn't automatically mean you'll get a better deal. Straight-sell salesmen usually have more experience in the business than the typical T.O. salesman. They can "nice" you to death if you aren't careful. Again, stick to the specific goals you have set for this particular visit to the dealership and escape when ready.

RULE NUMBER 4: BRING YOUR TRADE-IN WITH YOU THE FIRST TIME AND EVERY TIME

Common sense dictates that any time you add things together with a missing factor, your answer will be meaningless. Realize that when you get to the point where you're ready to gather price information, your trade is an integral part of the equation. Without a valid appraisal included in your price quote, you've completely wasted your time and effort. Still, buyers persist in shopping and pricing without their trade-in. They think it keeps them from buying a car. They think if they mention the trade-in at the last minute, they'll get a better deal. They won't, as we've already discussed.

Withholding this information gives the dealer a perfect way to quote totally misleading numbers. This touted practice of holding out the trade-in has become so commonplace that the dealer has learned how to work it to his advantage:

Q: I thought you said my car would be worth about fifty-five hundred dollars? What do you mean, now that you've seen it it's only worth four thousand?

A: Gee, sir, you didn't tell me it ———— (pick one or more: needs new tires, needs to be repainted, has so many miles, was such an ugly color, was this particular model, has a diesel engine, has door dings, has bird dung on the trunk, has dirty seatbelts).

Any used car will have some flaws, which one the dealer feels like making an issue of doesn't matter. If you accept anything short of a real appraisal on your car, this treatment is no one's fault but your own. Why put yourself through the drill? Concentrate on getting the information you need, not on being sneaky.

RULE NUMBER 5: SHOP AT PEAK TIMES WHEN SALESMEN AND MANAGERS ARE BUSY

This is one of the many differences between the domestic dealer and the import dealer. The domestic dealer can afford to roll one for the hell of it when things are slow, even if the profit involved is nearly nonexistent. It perks everyone up. It gives him a motivational story to tell at his next sales meeting. "If old Joe can sell a car at ten o'clock in the morning on a Tuesday, then by God all of you can!"

Not so with the import dealer.

Remember the allocation system? Sell one, no matter when, and you have one less to sell. Everyone has to count. When you hit the import dealer in an off-peak time, you haven't done yourself any favor. Quite the opposite; you find yourself faced with a fresh salesperson and a fresh manager who can take their time and work you to death.

What you want to do is hit the import dealer when he's up to his armpits in buyers, when he doesn't have time for games. If you come to him with a reasonable attitude and let him know exactly what you want to accomplish, he'll cooperate better with you at this point than at any other time.

When he's busy, he wants to sell cars and sell them with a minimum of strokes. He'll give you some reasonable numbers, appraise your car, and then let you walk, because there are a dozen other people standing around with no salesman to talk to, and he thinks they're all "today" buyers. He knows you're going to shop a few other dealers. He'll take his shot at you and then hope he sees you again. And that's exactly what you want to happen so you don't get mired down for three hours at every dealership you visit.

RULE NUMBER 6: BUY AT THE END OF THE MONTH, OR, MORE ACCURATELY, AT THE BEGINNING OF THE LAST FULL WEEK OF THE MONTH

There's a totally illogical but nonetheless real syndrome in the car business. It's called *make the month*. Suddenly, a salesman looks up at the status board and notices he's not going to make his quota. Or a sales manager sees that he's going to be short of his bonus by fifteen cars and he doesn't know where the buyers are going to come from.

They've been sitting there all month, holding grosses that would choke an alligator, and all of a sudden in the last moments of the month they realize how slow their rate of sale has been. It happens every month. The colored balloons come out of the back room and get tied to all of the used cars. The salesmen line up outside the sales manager's door with their crumpled notes and their unreadable worksheets and agonize over how to justify their jobs. The general manager sends out for more Rolaids and starts to leave his door open so he can listen to the activity on the floor. The calculators and the pencils come out of the desk drawers, and the average gross profits are examined to see just how close deals can be called without getting a call from the owner.

This is when you want to appear on the scene: one full week before the end of the month, so they know that you're deliverable before time runs out. Don't fail to point out to them that you'd like to get your shopping done in a hurry. Also, don't neglect to tell them that you're preapproved at your bank. Even if you decide to take one of their funny interest rates, at least they know that you're qualified up front.

RULE NUMBER 7: DON'T SWITCH MODELS AT THE LAST MINUTE

When a salesman can't make a deal because of price, a favorite tactic is to attempt to switch models on a buyer. Sometimes there will be a car available, the next model down from the one you're looking at, that has most of what you want in the way of equipment. Or perhaps it's one of last year's demonstrators with a few miles on it. Whatever the situation, the salesman will run it by you to see what your reaction will be before he gives up completely.

Be very careful here. There is the possibility that you're actually trying to buy too much car and that the substitute the salesman proposes to you really is a better way for you to go from a financial standpoint. But this isn't the car you've done your research on. This isn't the car you've established the market on. If you switch now, all of your hard work and preparation will go right out the window, and the ball will be in the dealer's court once again.

You'll be tired. You'll be eager to get all of the horsing around over with so you can stop spending the best part of your evenings in dealerships and the best part of your nights poring over the confusing numbers and packages. You'll also be more sensitive to price and payments than you are to a specific type of car. The model you're shown as an alternative might look better than you expect, given the difference in money. For most people, it's a real temptation to cave in, stop the game, and accept the lesser car.

My advice to you is to know what you can afford beforehand. Pick your car on the basis of whether you can swing it at full sticker. If you can, then proceed. If you can't, then realize what may happen to you if you find out you just can't get a dealer to negotiate a purchase price low enough to make that car fit your budget.

Realize that knowing the market on one particular model does not tell you anything about the market on similar models. A Volvo 740 turbo wagon will sell for a much different profit margin from a non-turbo-charged 740 wagon. A four-wheel-drive Honda wagon sells for a different profit margin from its look-alike two-wheel-drive version. If you decide to switch models, you'll have no choice but to start all over again.

RULE NUMBER 8: ALWAYS BE PLEASANT, BUT ALWAYS BE FIRM IN THE GOALS YOU'VE SET FOR THIS PARTICULAR VISIT TO THE DEALERSHIP

Salesmen, even the most jaded, appreciate someone who knows what he's after and doesn't create misleading impressions. If you tell him what you're after, and it turns out to be true, he'll be very pleasantly surprised. He may even reward your sincerity with more information than you expect.

Salesmen deal with hostile, frightened, distrustful people seven days a week. If you're direct and friendly, you stand a chance of putting a few of them off their guard.

RULE NUMBER 9: MAKE A HABIT OF DOING EXACTLY WHAT YOU SAY YOU'LL DO

This goes hand in hand with rule number 8, but it deserves expansion because it's such a critical point. What I'm talking about is your credibility as a buyer.

How many times have you told a salesman you were just looking when you were actually in the final stages of serious car shopping?

How many times have you told the salesman you couldn't afford the payments he just quoted you, when you knew full well that you could and what you really wanted was a better deal?

How many times have you told a salesman you were going to shop three dealers for a price without telling them what his particular price quote was, and then blatantly proceeded to use his price as a lever to lower each succeeding dealer's bid?

How many times have you told a dealer that there would be no trade-in to consider, and then at the last moment "changed your mind"?

How many times have you told a dealer that you weren't ready to buy because you had just started shopping, when actually he was the eighth dealer you'd been to that day alone?

How many times have you told a salesman that his deal sounded good but that you would have to think about it overnight, knowing full well that you'd already decided not to buy a car from him?

How many times have you signed a retail purchase order, supposedly in good faith, and then used your order to shop every other dealer in the state?

How many times have you failed to ask for a salesman who'd already spent some of his time with you, when you promised him that you would?

This is only a partial listing, but I think by now I've made my point. Is it any wonder that salesmen attempt to maneuver you into buying a car on your first visit to their dealership? Is it any wonder that they sometimes ignore what you tell them and keep asking you to buy their car?

Here's a new wrinkle. If you do this right, you will go to the dealer at least three times before you sign your retail purchase order. First, to talk about cars only; second, to get a price quote and trade-in appraisal for comparison purposes; and third, to make your buying offer. If you've told your salesman each time you've seen him exactly what you were doing and why (and I recommend making appointments with specific salesmen), then he will be able to go to his manager and tell him that you have done exactly what you have said you would at each step of the process. You will have built credibility where none usually exists. So, now that you have credibility, what good is it? I'll tell you.

Every time you actually do what you say you will, it becomes easier to leave the dealership without a lot of last-ditch histrionics. If you say you'll be back, they believe it. Every time you return on schedule they're more convinced you've learned what the market is on the car in question. Every time they deal with you they're less likely to play games with you. When you make your offer to purchase, they're going to believe there's a dealer out there who's close to your figure. If you happen to be on the bottom of their gross profit criteria, you will have bought yourself a car. You will have won the game.

The slogan in the business is "buyers are liars"; why not distinguish yourself?

RULE NUMBER 10: NEVER BUY ON THE FIRST VISIT TO THE DEALERSHIP

Without comparison shopping you're getting your facts from a magician. If you want to be fooled, there are less expensive and more entertaining ways to have it done than in an automobile dealership.

RULE NUMBER 11: REMEMBER, THE DEALER WHO PROTESTS THE LOUDEST YOUR INTENTION TO COMPARISON-SHOP IS, MOST LIKELY, THE DEALER WITH THE HIGHEST PRICE

For visit number one, when you're still shopping kinds of cars and your salesman wants to talk price:

■ "I can appreciate what you're saying, but I'm still trying to decide what kind of a car I want to buy. There's no need to talk about pricing until I know for sure it's your car I actually want."

■ "There are two elements in a price, aren't there: cost and value? Instead of talking about cost would you mind showing some of the features of your car that give it value?"

■ "The more quickly I learn about your car, the more quickly I'll be ready to buy."

For visit number two, when your salesman wants you to buy right now and you haven't found out what the market really is on the car you want:

■ "If your pricing is as competitive as you say it is, then my comparison shopping will only bear that out, isn't that right?"

■ "I always comparison-shop before I buy anything, and I'm always glad I did."

▪ "I can appreciate the fact that it would be to your benefit if I bought your car today, but you must appreciate that it's to my benefit to learn what the market value of your product is before I buy. As a professional, would you do less?"

And as long as you deliver your lines with good humor, don't worry about being offensive. Good salesmen appreciate good technique.

RULE NUMBER 12: DON'T LIE, THE DEALER IS INFINITELY BETTER AT IT ANYWAY

We've already talked about how foolish it is to expect a dealer to believe phony price information. Along the same lines, if you tell him another dealer has a certain car in stock when he doesn't, it's all too easy for him to check your story out by having his manager give that dealer a quick call on the pretense of a dealer trade. Your salesman and his manager will know you lied to them before you ever leave the dealership. Pinpointing inventory for a dealer is always dangerous anyway. If the dealer needs the unit you've so kindly located for him, you might get that unit traded out from under you. I've seen it happen.

RULE NUMBER 13: DON'T WORK WITH "BALLPARK" FIGURES

Salesmen love ballpark figures. This practice is an open invitation to mislead you into thinking you can buy a car for less at their particular dealership than you actually can. It's more polite than a blatant lowball and it can be more easily handled when the buyer returns. Remember, ballpark figures are only meant to give you an idea. Who's to say how big the ballpark is?

Ballpark figures are also the lazy way out. People who think they can avoid being "set upon" by fourteen different closers by cornering their salesman on the demo ride and then refusing to sit at his desk when they return to the dealership are lazy. People who are afraid to get close to anything that resembles a selling situation because they think the salesman has some mystical power that will force them to buy a car before they're ready are simply wrong.

If you expect to get a good deal, you're going to have to expend some effort.

9

SCOUTING REPORTS

The next thing on the agenda is to take a close look inside the dealership, and its inside sales technique in general. This time we're going to follow the salesman into the manager's office and observe what really goes on in there; why the salesman says the things he does; what actual maneuvers are employed to try to sell you a car. In the simplest possible terms, what we're going to do is "scout" the opposing team to learn some of its offensive plays and tactics, because knowing the offense helps you to play better defense.

However, keep in mind that spotting a sales tactic and getting upset at the dealer won't win the game for you. Fighting the dealer's system won't get you a better deal, and trying to force the dealer to "play it your way" will only cause you frustration. You will learn some basic selling techniques in this chapter, and you'll learn some countermoves, but the key to success in this endeavor remains the same: obtain accurate market information *and only then* accept a purchase price in the lower ranges of that market value. It's really that simple. You may think, after you've studied this chapter, that you've suddenly learned how to "win the argument" with the dealer. In some cases this may be true, but it only means you'll have to buy your car somewhere else. In sales, no one wins an argument, neither the buyer nor the seller.

Let's start by paying homage to the five most powerful words in sales of any type, and certainly of sales in the car business.

"IF I COULD, WOULD YOU?"

Armed with this little phrase alone, and the willingness to work sixty to seventy hours a week, you too could be making $50,000 per year in the car business. You don't need a master's degree in marketing, or even a college education. All you need is a little practice in when to ask this pregnant question.

"If I had a car in stock you like, would you buy it today?"

"If I could save you enough money, would you buy a car today?"

"If I could get your payments down another $10 a month, could you swing it then?"

"If I could get you another $500 on your trade, could we make a deal today?"

"If I could find a five-speed in this model, would you want it?"

"Now that we've made a deal, if there were a way I could save you $50 a month on your car payment (that is, lease conversion), would you be interested?"

Any of the above sound familiar? You bet it does. You've already heard this particular baited hook a zillion times. In some dealerships, and with some salesmen, a version of this question will amount to 50 percent of your total conversation. It's the blunt instrument of choice for "green peas" and veterans alike. Why? Because it works.

This little phrase has committed more buyers to buy before they were ready than any other means going. If you say yes to an "If I could, would you?" question, your only way out is to lie and seemingly go back on your word. That's why it works so well.

So how do you avoid this question? Simple. You give the salesman something he wants, but not exactly what he asked for. For example:

Q: If I have a car in stock you like, would you buy it today?
A: I hope to buy a car by the end of the month.
Q: If I could save you enough money, would you buy a car today?
A: After I've done some comparison shopping, I don't know of any reason we can't do business.
Q: If I could get your payments down another ten dollars a month, could you swing it then?
A: I'm sure I could swing it whether you could reduce the payments by another ten dollars or not, but that's not the point. Should I do my comparison shopping on the basis of your first set of numbers or on the lower figures?

(Take special note of this. Here the tactic is assumed consent; it's an exercise in blurring the lines. If you say yes to the question, your salesman will automatically understand you to mean that you will buy the car today if he can arrange a $10-a-month lower payment. He'll get up from his desk quickly and charge off to his manager's office before you have a chance to think. After he comes back from his visit to the sales manager, he will act very upset with you when you tell him that what you meant was that a $10-a-month lower payment would naturally fit your budget better and not that you had conditionally agreed to buy a car on the spot. You must meet this tactic head-on by redefining the question in definite terms. Tell him what he just said, before he comes back and tells you what *you* just said.)

One final point: the natural tendency is to answer an "If I could, would you?" question with either a yes or a no. From our examples you can see that it's to your benefit to avoid this inclination. Instead, keep stating your goals for this particular visit to the dealership. Give the salesman a reason to continue talking with you, but don't surrender all of your flexibility and maneuvering room by allowing yourself to be limited to strict yes or no answers. Expand on your answer until your meaning is clear.

THE MYTH OF THE SALESMAN WHO'S "IN THERE WORKING FOR YOU"—AND WHY YOU WANT SO BADLY TO BELIEVE IT'S TRUE

Salesmen work for dealerships, not for customers. When a salesman wants a new demonstrator, or a draw against his next week's commission check, does he call you up on the phone? If he negotiates a lower price than usual for you, does it somehow make him more money than he would normally earn from the sale? Do dealerships give bonuses for low gross deals? Why, then, do so many people persist in their belief that the salesman is their "friend in the car business" and will look after their best interest?

Granted, it's a scary situation to be in, especially when you really don't know what's going on and all you want to do is buy a new car. You really do need some advice from someone knowledgeable to keep you from getting nailed to the wall (or "laid away," as the saying goes). But the salesman isn't that someone. Making him your trusted adviser is the best definition of conflict of interest I can think of.

When you start off you have a lot of very healthy fears and reservations about trusting any salesman. But the situation tends to change rapidly once the faceless demon becomes a real person with real pictures of his wife and kids displayed on his desk. You'll gradually find yourself relaxing. You'll begin to grant credibility to what this individual has to say.

Dealerships intentionally hire people with very pleasant

personalities to sell their cars. They know it's next to impossible for you to distrust someone you like. Realize something though; the salesman is there for one reason: to sell you a car for as much money as he can get you to pay for it. The minute he gets confused and starts working for his customers, he's out of a job.

And it's a good job, one he doesn't want to lose. I've seen too many people make too much money as car salesmen to believe they would risk it all for the well-being of one customer.

THE ACADEMY AWARDS FOR SINCERITY

It's been said that in sales sincerity is everything—and that if you can learn to fake sincerity you've got it made. This may sound like a very jaded statement to make, but it's true. The effectiveness of anything a salesman says is directly proportional to the degree of sincerity of his delivery. But, of course, just because what a salesman says may sound like the truth, it ain't necessarily so, which is certainly the case with the top-flight import salesman.

To make matters worse for the import buyer, there are a growing number of highly skilled individuals making the rounds and educating the auto salesman in a cornucopia of different areas. Fortunes are being made by professional sales trainers who attempt to teach salesmen how to, among other things, seem more sincere in their presentation and in their closing techniques. Among the varied skills the average salesman is now exposed to on a repeated basis are the following:

■ Matching emotional levels with a buyer. If you're reserved in your demeanor, he'll be reserved. If you're boisterous, his presentation will be more animated.

■ Asking questions that lead you along in the most beneficial direction for his purposes. He who asks the questions is in control.

■ Confirming statements you make that tend to strengthen his case. You say, "That's a nice-looking car"; he says, "It *is* one of the nicest-looking cars on the road today, isn't it?"

■ Using conversation-building techniques such as "piggy-backing," or formulating a new question on the basis of the answer to the question just asked. (He asks, "Where do you work?" You say, "XYZ Corporation." He says, "Gee, I'm not familiar with that company. What do they do?" You say, "Engineering work." He says, "Are you an engineer, then?" Pretty soon he has you talking about a subject you're both knowledgeable about and comfortable with. Automatically you relax and, more important to the salesman, your guard starts to come down.)

As you can see, there's a lot of expertise in sales beyond the simple "If I could, would you?": contrived sincerity, artful conversation management, covert mind-focusing techniques. Indeed, an accomplished salesman can be a formidable person to reckon with unless you have a well-thought-out game plan and keep your goals clearly in mind. If only you could judge your salesman ahead of time, so you would know just how well he'd learned his craft, or so you could avoid the super-stars.

Guess what? You can.

Salespeople of all types are competitive people. They like to outdistance their fellow workers and they respond to recognition. Sales managers—motivators by their own definition—play on this competitive strain by producing an endless flood of wood and brass plaques. These are the salesman-of-the-month awards that decorate at least one wall of every automobile dealership in the known world. Salesmen often call them "Wooden Attaboys"; I call them the "Academy Awards for Sincerity." Want to know who you're up against? Go read the wall.

Of course, this is one of the absurdities of the car business, and a lot of other sales businesses as well. If we were at war with each other, would I tell you who my best marksmen were? If I were a casino owner in Las Vegas, would I clearly mark the slot machines that pay off the fewest amount of times for their players? This sort of thing should be classified information, not put on display. It's nuts, but that doesn't stop you from taking advantage of it.

THE "UP" SYSTEM AND HOW IT KEEPS YOU FROM PICKING YOUR OWN SALESMAN, MUCH TO YOUR DISADVANTAGE

Unfortunately, even if you ran into the dealership, executed your very best broken field running, found your way to the "wall of honor," and managed to identify the guy at the very bottom of the heap, in most dealerships it still wouldn't do you any good. That's because of floor protocol. Salesmen generally rotate, much as a batting order rotates; hence the often-heard cry from across the showroom floor when a new customer appears on the lot: "Who's up?"

Naturally, there's a good deal of emotion expressed over the whole issue of which salesman you rightfully belong to. Salesmen who repeatedly go out of rotation are called some very colorful names such as lot lizard, floor whore, and skate. Be that as it may, the "up" system stops you from picking your own salesman.

WOMEN IN THE BUSINESS

The car business used to be male dominated, but not anymore. And if you believe a woman salesperson is going to be softer on you in a deal, think again. Face it, auto sales is a personality business, and most women have had more training in this area. I've worked with three women salespersons. Each one was a sales leader. Three for three—that's a perfect batting average. Think about that one.

THE REAL REASON FOR THE MANAGER/ SALESMAN STRUCTURE OF MOST DEALERSHIPS, AND WHAT YOU CAN DO ABOUT IT

Believe it or not, salesmen get trapped by buyers from time to time. The buyer plays his own game of "If I would, could you?" or he makes a confusing offer, or he tricks the salesman into telling him what a minimal deal actually consists of. There are inept salesmen out there. Even the best of the lot feels the pressure of the selling situation.

Enter the sales manager. If a salesman makes twenty deals in a month, a sales manager makes two hundred. After a while he knows by heart the cost of every car well enough to detect it when the figures are off. And he has the luxury of sitting at his desk in his quiet little chamber and analyzing the ingredients in front of him. He can fiddle with the recipe unfettered until he comes up with a workable combination. He can call up his wholesaler and quiz him about the trade without being overheard by the buyer. He can look over a credit application and determine whether the buyer has enough of a down payment to be financeable. Above all, he can compare notes with his salesman, read the salesman's level of confidence and take a quick sounding of where he thinks the deal is, and decide which way to proceed.

Learning to do anything is a function of how much thought you put into the thing you're trying to do and how often you get to do it. If the sales manager sees ten times the deals the salesman does, he in fact has ten times the experience. This means that your salesman is only 10 percent, or less, of your problem. Chances are that it will be the sales manager who calls the play in and not the salesman. It's the

salesman's responsibility to execute; only rarely will he inno-
vate.

Let's take a look at the salesman's agenda:

■ Establish a line of communication with the buyer; get
him to think of you as a human being.
■ Find a specific car he wants to buy. People get excited
only when things get specific.
■ Gather the basic ingredients of the deal: down payment, type of trade, buy or lease, monthly budget, basic
creditworthiness, time frames.
■ Obtain a commitment to buy the car under specific
conditions—"If I could, would you?"
■ Bring the deal to the manager's desk for approval and/or
counteroffer, and follow instructions.

Notice that the salesman hasn't committed himself or his
dealership to a thing. You've supplied the information and the
starting point for negotiations. The salesman may have tried
to condition you to a certain price or payment level, and
certainly to a trade-in value (high, high, and low, respec-
tively), but he hasn't put anything on the table for you to
accept or reject. Nor will he, in the beginning.

Even though, ordinarily you don't have the faintest idea
of what the market is on the car you're trying to buy, you'll be
asked to "appraise" it. You'll be asked to set a value with
virtually nothing to go on but perhaps the unsubstantiated
rumors of people you work with, or the neighbor down the
street (who might have bought last year's model for all you
know). You don't know if you've started your negotiations
high or low. You'll only know that your initial offer isn't
acceptable. And you can count on that; it will *always* be too
low.

Here's the kicker: even if your offer is well within the
market range of the car you are trying to buy, the dealer will

initially reject it. His aim? Maximize profit! It's also bad psychology to accept the first offer. Nothing frightens a veteran salesman more than writing a deal based on the buyer's first set of numbers. He knows that, unless this car is spot-delivered, at some point on the drive home the buyer will wonder if he should have perhaps made a lower offer after all, and he'll decide to see just one more dealer.

If the buyer does this, the salesman knows he can forget that deal, or at the very least be faced with having to renegotiate. It's far better to make the buyer work for his discount. Make him sit and sweat it out, then he'll be too tired, and too unwilling, to go through the process again with another dealer for at least three years.

So, what happens next? Your dashing salesman has disappeared into the sales manager's office. He's been in there for ten minutes. What's taking so long, anyway? Do they have to call overseas to get permission from the manufacturer to sell a car?

THE FALSE BOTTOM

Sadly, most buyers either don't shop at all or shop ineffectively. For example, they might gather ballpark figures or negotiate with two dealers of different makes of cars. If you got a hard price from a Toyota dealer and then did the same from a Honda dealer, what would either figure tell you about the market on either car?

This opens the door for some creative showmanship and a possible nomination for an Academy Award for Sincerity. I'm talking about creating the presumption of a good price.

I don't know if anyone's ever sat down and formalized the procedure I'm about to describe to you. I didn't learn about it in a seminar, or even in a sales meeting; I learned it through selling several hundred cars. The increments themselves will vary from sales manager to sales manager, but the concept remains the same. It's very simple, as you will see, and yet

very effective. If I've failed thus far to convince you to comparison-shop before you buy your next new car, this should
dispel any doubts.

How do you know when you're getting to the end of the
available discount on the car you're trying to buy? Think
about it. The salesman stays longer and longer in the sales
manager's office before he comes back. Each successive price
concession is smaller than the one that preceded it. Before
long, you're down to two-digit numbers. Finally, the salesman who can't get you to raise your offer, or his manager to
lower his any more, offers to buy you a set of floormats out of
his own pocket to close the deal. Whoopee! What a deal you
got on this one! And free floormats to boot!

Sure.

Before you OD on euphoria and self-congratulations, let
me ask you one question. If the sales manager had $1,500 to
work with until he reached the bottom of the market on his
car, what's to stop him from holding out $500 or $600? What's
to stop him from getting down into the single-digit phase of
your negotiation when he's given away $900 instead of $1,400?

Look at it this way:

First drop	$500
Second drop	$200
Third drop	$100
Fourth drop	$50
Fifth drop	floormats

After spending four hours in the dealership and going
through five offers and counteroffers, having your trade appraised twice, your credit application studied by the sales
manager and the finance manager, perhaps being turned over
to another salesman to boot, you'll feel as if you've made a
fairly good deal.

However, no matter how sincerely the salesman offers to
buy you floormats, if you have a price from another dealer

that's $600 lower, you aren't going to fall for it. Even if the salesman's sincerity is absolutely genuine—and it could be, if he hasn't been told by his sales manager how much of a gross profit is being held at the moment—*no one can fool you if you know the market*.

THE "OLD-PRICED" CAR GAME

As we've discussed before, price increases on import cars have run rampant for the last several years, with sometimes four and five individual increases during a single model year. This means that at certain times there may be a real disparity between prices from different dealers, even given the same profit margin.

When a price increase occurs, a sales manager with only fresh inventory to sell sits and steams until the last of the lower-priced cars his competing dealers may have in stock are sold. He knows that for a while he won't sell any cars to the comparison shoppers, who naturally will find the cars with the built-in price advantage. Fortunately for him, these cars tend to disappear quickly, though, and then it's business as usual. However, there is one variation on this theme that you should watch for.

Obviously, the dealer who is holding back cars to maximize his profits will be the dealer left with the most lower-priced cars at any given time. This is the one time when the manufacturers' suggested retail price is a more relevant piece of information than the dealer's add-on sticker because there is nothing to keep the dealer from "equalizing" his prices. In other words, use the same add-on sticker total price on both new- and old-priced cars. This makes the lower-priced car even more profitable for the dealer because the higher figures will be used across-the-board. It also makes it easier for him to sell one of these cars, because he has more room to negotiate on its price while holding the same gross profit margin.

And then there's the demonstrator. Most people buy

demonstrators to save money. They expect the dealer to sell his demonstrators for a smaller profit margin because they are "functionally" used cars and less desirable than a fresh unit with no accumulated mileage. Of course, the demonstrator has been around for a while, hasn't it? And that means it could fall very easily into the formerly priced category. In fact, if there has been more than one price increase during the model year, a demonstrator could conceivably be one, two, or even three prices old. At my last dealership we had so many old-priced cars around at one point, both new and demonstrators, that we had to color-code the stock cards to keep from getting confused.

A word to the wise: look at the manufacturers' suggested retail price on like models on the dealer's lot. There's no reason to give the dealer $300 or $400 extra profit he hasn't earned.

THE PRACTICE OF WAREHOUSING BUYERS

We've given a lot of space to the dealer who holds back his inventory in order to maximize his profits. As profitable as this practice is for the dealer who can get away with it, hiding cars takes a tremendous amount of money to pull off on a regular basis. Approximately $100,000 is tied up for every ten cars a dealer keeps in inventory, whether the money comes out of his pocket or is borrowed from the bank on his floor plan. Hold just fifty cars and you're flirting with $500,000 out of pocket. This is the big reason not all dealers play this particular game. They just can't afford the table stakes.

There is another operating philosophy that works nearly as well, however. It has the advantage of requiring less money. It's called *warehousing buyers.*

Suppose you have more than one buyer lined up—contract signed, deposit already in your bank account—for every car coming into your dealership. This means that as soon as each car rolls off the transporter it gets prepped for delivery;

no delays, no standing inventory to speak of. What would you gain?

For one thing, you'd have a zero floor plan expense. You'd also have a lot of money sitting in your bank, interest free, courtesy of your customers. Let's do a little arithmetic: say the dealer requires a $500 deposit on ordered cars, and he currently holds a hundred deposits. That's $50,000 to play with. Not enough to retire on, but certainly not peanuts, either. I know one dealer who boasts that he carries up to four hundred deposits at any one given time.

Now give some thought to the following scenario. Because of his ultracompetitive pricing, a dealer sells out his allocation ahead of time for the next several months, but the buyers still keep coming. The dealer begins to edge up his gross profit margin on each successive sale because he knows he's covered anyway. Why not do a little profit maximizing? Still the buyers keep coming. Suddenly he has more buyers than he has incoming cars left in his allocation. What does he do?

He keeps on taking deposits, because it's free money and because ultimately people get impatient and drop out, or their situation changes, or they mess up their credit. Ever had a car on order for six months and still get a call saying you'll have to look at next year's allocation because the factory has told the dealer they can't fill your order before the end of the current model year's production? I've made those calls, and they aren't any fun. Ever wonder how in the world this could have happened when you ordered your car so early in the model year?

Here's another maxim for you: the only good deal you can get is on a "real" car. Buy cars in stock. Buy cars on a legitimate incoming allocation, and get ID numbers. Buy a car on a locate basis with a time limit. Don't leave your situation open-ended. It will only cost you money. I've never seen anyone yet who could drive a purchase order to work.

THE CLOSER

Whether it's the salesman you've been working with all along, as will be the case in the straight-sell-type dealership, or a separate individual into whose office you are led and then abandoned by your salesman, as is often the case at the turnover dealership, the closer should not frighten you. Good closers as a rule are very pleasant, personable individuals who know something of human nature and have mastered a few of the common closing techniques. If you've done your preparation, you aren't overmatched at all; he is.

He is going to do certain things that usually don't vary much from dealer to dealer. First, he's going to try to make you comfortable. He'll tell you to have a seat; he'll offer you a cup of coffee. Then he's going to attempt to humanize himself in your eyes. He'll talk about anything and everything but the car you want to buy and the price you want to pay. Only when you are sufficiently relaxed will he proceed with the matter at hand.

Now, before he talks about numbers, he'll try to determine whether or not the salesman has done his job of finding the car you want to buy. He'll ask you plainly enough if you like the car in question. He may ask you why, so he knows firsthand what the strongest points of his product are in your eyes. Each time you make a positive statement, he'll play the confirmation game with you by restating each of your positive points with what are called *tie downs* (tie downs are the little expressions such as "isn't it," "doesn't it," "can't you"). Finally, he'll start clarifying the numbers, and out will come the closing techniques as you begin to object.

There are only a few closing techniques in use, but unfortunately each one has about a billion variations. Let's take a brief look at some of the more popular ones.

The order blank close. Once the closer determines that you like the car you've been shown, he takes out his retail order form and begins to fill it out. He keeps on filling it out, simply asking you the questions on the form pertaining to name, address, model, color, stock number, and so forth, until you stop him. If you don't stop him, he'll turn the completed purchase order around and ask you to "approve it," "autograph it," or "write your name on it"—he'll say anything except "sign it." *Sign it* are supposedly frightening words, to be avoided at all costs. (Buyers apparently aren't supposed to be smart enough to know that approving an agreement is the same thing as signing a contract.)

This is by far the most popular first attempt to close—or, in sales parlance, the *trial close*. It usually tells the closer just how near you are to making a deal. If you stop him right after he writes the date on his form, he knows he's in trouble; this is just what I suggest you do.

Reduce to the ridiculous. Here the closer takes your objection, usually either total price or monthly payments, and breaks it down to increments that become increasingly silly.

"You say the payment is too much? How much too much? Ten dollars a month? Do you realize that ten dollars a month is only two-fifty a week, thirty-three cents a day, one-point-four cents an hour? You mean you'd turn down the car of your dreams for a piddling penny an hour?"

The closer's goal here is to take the weight out of your price objection and make you feel a little foolish about it. This technique quite often gets some movement from a buyer even before the deal is taken to the sales manager. What you should do is turn the closer's telescope around and have him look through the other end. "Do you realize that ten dollars a month adds up to six hundred dollars over the course of a five-year loan? I do." If you do it with a smile on your face he won't be offended; he'll also know that attempting to "preshrink" your price objections is a waste of his time.

Recognize, sympathize, and minimize. Here the closer will carefully restate your objection to show you he's actually listened to you and understands what you've said. Then he'll tell you, very sincerely, that if he were you he might feel the same way. Finally, he'll attempt to minimize the power of your objections by offering you a compromise with an "If I could, would you?" type of question. Once their grievances have been fully aired, a large percentage of buyers will agree to a compromise position almost immediately.

Closing on a minor point. I once had a sales manager who was very fond of telling his salespeople that it was impossible to be "10 percent shot in the head." You either were shot or you weren't. As true as this is, buyers seem to prefer to be shot in the head 10 percent rather than 100 percent. What I mean is this: instead of asking a buyer directly if he will buy the car, a good closer can be expected to ask a question about something minor that, if answered, assumes buying the car as a prerequisite. Such as: "Will you or your spouse be driving the new car home?" "Would you prefer a set of free floormats to make the deal, or would you rather have the protective wheel well trim?" "Would you like thirty or forty-five days until your first payment?" or "Do you want the new car registered in just one or both of your names?"

The point is, don't worry about these minor questions until you've settled the major one. Keep in mind that it's impossible to be 10 percent shot in the head.

The modified "puppy dog" close, or the "Polaroid" close. Years ago, when cars weren't so expensive, a dealer might offer to let a buyer take a new car home overnight while he considered whether to buy it or not. What would often happen was that the buyer would end up showing off the new car to his family and his neighbors. As a result, the dealer's car would very quickly become the buyer's car in his mind, and the motivation to close the deal would be substantially heightened.

The key element here is establishing a tangible connection between the car and the customer. If the customer could be made to identify himself with the new car, closing him when he came back the next day would be short work. After all, who wants to "lose" their new car over a few dollars?

Nowadays, if you can't make up your mind, don't be surprised to see the Polaroid come out and to have a picture snapped of you while you are carefully posed beside the car of your dreams. Suddenly you can really see yourself owning that new car. You're sure to show the picture to your friends and family. "Oh, is that your new car? When do you pick it up?"

Be careful how you answer.

What's your defense for all of these tactics? How do you keep from being swept away by the hypnotic spell of the "super-closer"? You can probably recite the answer by now—once again, with feeling—*If you've done your preparation and if you know the market on the car you are trying to buy, no one can fool you into paying more. You are the one who signs your checks. Without your consent, no one can sell you anything. Remember your specific goals for this particular visit to the dealership, and don't be afraid to remind your salesman what they are.*

Remember, too, that good humor goes a long way, even with salesmen. That way they'll be glad to see you when you come back.

WHEN AND HOW TO ALLOW YOURSELF TO BE CLOSED

Ultimately you will know the market on the car you're trying to buy. You'll be truly ready to make your offer in earnest and actually buy that brand-new car. So what do you do at this point? Cruise into the dealership and ask for your keys?

I'm sorry to disappoint you, but you still have a little more work to do, and it's critical that you do it right.

For the very same reason that the dealer is unlikely to accept a buyer's first offer, you can't afford to simply go back to the dealer who gave you the lowest set of figures and tell him to write it up. It gives the dealer far too much leverage. Here's what I mean: Sales managers are pathological negotiators. Once they have a position, they can't resist trying to improve it. If they have a $4,000 gross profit in a deal, they try to get it up to $4,250. But, of course, they have to be careful; no buyer likes to be raised, or "bumped," after the fact, and a good many buyers are presensitized to this maneuver from years of buying domestic cars.

Still, sales managers know that you've gone to a lot of effort to comparison-shop. You're probably near your limit of tolerance for the whole game and more than a little anxious to get it over with. And, of course, the fact that you're back tells them something else that most of them find irksome; all of the other dealers you shopped were holding slightly higher gross profits. Why not, the rationale goes, try and even up things a bit? No one likes to think he's the weak link, certainly not a salesman.

It's imperative to make the dealer work for your deal. It's the only bump insurance available to you.

Remember when you were a small child and you saw a really juicy cupcake sitting all alone on the counter? It was right there for the taking, and no one was around to stop you—but you just weren't quite tall enough to reach it. The moment you realized that you might not be able to get your hands on it, all of a sudden you wanted that cupcake more badly than anything. You'd stretch and strain, go find a book or a toy to stand on, or offer to split the spoils with an older brother or sister. At the point when you thought you couldn't have what you wanted, your motivation peaked. This is what you have to do to the sales manager when you go back to place your order. You have to take his position away from him momentarily. You have to put some doubts in his head.

Even though you know what the actual market is on the car in question, and even though you know that it's very unlikely the dealer will go below this figure, in order to protect yourself from being bumped, you're going to offer the dealer something *slightly* less than market for his car. Not much less, just $200 or $300 or so.

Then sit back and listen to all the sales and closing techniques until you feel you've put them through their paces. Allow yourself to be closed at, or perhaps slightly below, what you've found to be the market value on your car.

The common thread in all negotiation is compromise. Take advantage of this fact for once, instead of having the salesman take advantage of *you* with it. "Engineer" the compromise you want by anticipating what the sales manager will do. But, don't, under any circumstances, tell the dealer you have "the deal" at another place. Be forthright and tell him that your offer is—simply what you want to pay for his car—then compromise at market. Remember, any competent sales manager can spot a phony price almost immediately.

Warning: if you play this game too hard on an incoming or locate-type car, you may run the risk of getting "warehoused." You have to negotiate, but don't go overboard. Be sure to play the hardest for cars that are in stock. Use the dealer's immediate-delivery psychology for your own purposes.

On a personal note, I'm very glad I'm not selling cars for a living anymore. For one thing, at this point I wouldn't want to meet up with *you* as a buyer!

10

JUST ONE MORE THING

So, now you've done it. For the first time in your car-buying experience you've come to the market prepared. You know you've negotiated a fair deal without having those nagging doubts, or without the fear that old Harry will laugh at you at your next cocktail party and tell you how he bought his car for a grand less than you did. It took a little work and some preparation, granted, but you managed to keep some of your money for other things because of it. Congratulations. There's "just this one thing," as Columbo used to say.

Suddenly we're faced with a "catch-22." Many of the very same things you've had to do to get the right price on your new car now become a hindrance to a proper delivery. You're at the very peak of the end-of-the-month rush. The sales manager is turning up the heat on your salesman to make sure your financing really is set—you handled it yourself, remember? The service department is trying to figure out just how they're going to get a zillion cars prepped and cleaned in a fraction of the time they actually need to do the job thoroughly. The delivery coordinator or F&I person is still miffed at you because you didn't buy anything from him.

In short, there aren't many things more absurd than the only tacitly organized chaos a dealer goes through once a month, and you've put yourself squarely in the middle of it.

"But," you say, "it is a new car, isn't it; fresh, right from the factory, perfect in every way? And the dealer is a professional who's delivered thousands of cars. Why should I worry?"

This is a time to be very cool and calm. This isn't a baby being delivered here, and you're under no moral obligation to take whatever appears and love it no matter what. This is one time it's advisable to look over your item *very closely* before you take it home.

WHY YOU SHOULD KNOW THE ORIGINS OF YOUR NEW CAR

Of course, you know who made your new car. (We're going to ignore, for the moment, the fact that some Swedish cars are actually made in Belgium and Canada, that some Japanese and some German cars are put together in the United States. Let's not even talk about what's going on in Mexico.) What you should primarily be concerned with here is what's happened to your car since it left the factory. These are the "origins" we need to talk about.

Stop and think about this for a minute. If your "new" car actually came from overseas, without doubt it's been driven a number of times and by a number of people who had no ownership interest in it. What I'm saying is, it's had plenty of opportunity to get damaged or abused along the way. It was driven from the factory to a holding area, eventually loaded onto a transport, and hauled in the open to another holding area at the dock where it was unloaded and parked. Then it was driven on to what is commonly referred to as a *Ro Ro*, meaning roll-on, roll-off, ship. Then the ship bounced and vibrated it for thousands of miles, through many kinds of weather, to another holding area, another truck ride, perhaps a supplemental holding area, another truck ride, and, ultimately, the dealer's lot.

Now I ask you, is there a chance that someone, somewhere along this odyssey, has accidently scratched, dinged, dented, or otherwise violated your prize? You bet. Spend some time examining your new car before you drive it off the lot.

"OFF THE TRUCK"

The very best you can do for yourself is to get a unit right off the truck. The main reason for this is that virtually all of the manufacturers set limits on how much shipping damage they'll allow a dealer to accept. Some limits are as low as $300, and if you've been to a body shop recently you know that $300 doesn't buy much paint anymore. What the manufacturers are trying to accomplish is to establish quality controls as well as to minimize unusual exposure to warranty claims. Naturally this policy helps you, because it goes a long way toward guaranteeing that your new car hasn't been extensively reworked without your knowledge. Unfortunately, there are a number of ways the dealer can circumvent the best intentions of the manufacturer if doing so happens to suit his situation.

Suppose for a moment that you're a dealer. You've been waiting for a while for a hard-to-get model to come in for one of your customers. You stand to make $3,000 or $4,000 if you can deliver this unit before you lose your sale because of the impatience of your buyer. Your competition has been beating your prices all month. Your top salesman has gone on vacation. Your sales manager is over his ad budget again. Then, suddenly, the truck arrives and you spot your high-gross unit gleaming from the top rails of the trailer. Eagerly, you watch as the truck driver begins to back it off. Then it happens: an improperly placed ramp slips, and your unit crunches down on its frame rails.

You can't see the damage unless you look under the car, but the manufacturer's policy is clear—no cars are to be accepted with frame damage of any kind. The truck driver is comatose; he knows he's probably lost his job. The salesman involved in the deal is deathly white; he's already spent his commission. And you can see $4,000 blowing down the road to a competing dealer's store.

If, that is, you choose to "see" the damage. After all, there's always the possibility that your customer will run over something on the way home and think *he* caused the damage.

Ask any dealer, or salesman, or truck driver who carries automobiles if something very similar to this has ever happened to him, and watch how quickly they take the Fifth Amendment.

The fact is, the vast majority of cars come through without a scratch, but enough of them are damaged and then repaired for it to be a legitimate concern for the import buyer. All I suggest is that you open your eyes and take a realistic look. If there is an appropriate time for a "third baseman," time of delivery is it; sometimes impartial eyes see through the mist a good deal better.

THE "IN-STOCK" UNIT

What about the "in-stock" unit? After all, you can't be expected to hang around the dealership for weeks just to make sure you personally see your car roll safely off the truck.

Logically, the in-stock unit is the next best thing to a unit straight off the truck, but there are other possibilities to consider. The first is that few dealers keep their inventory under cover. (If you live in an area prone to hail, you might want to take special note.) Second, there's the myth of the demo. Salesmen, much to the dealer's consternation, aren't very good housekeepers when it comes to the demonstrator they are given to drive. They also don't like to have every Tom, Dick, and Harry out driving around on their gas—yes, these days the salesman probably buys his own gas. The salesman's solution is (1) not to keep much more than fumes in his tank at any given time, and (2) to encourage his customers to drive a "fresh" unit from inventory. Thus, most new cars are demonstrated to more than one buyer before they are sold. This means that the lines drawn between a demonstrator that's been officially subjected to the abuse of the public at large and a "new" unit are particularly blurry. Keep in mind that if it's sitting on the lot, it's been driven; and if it's been driven, it may have also been driven to the body shop. I've seen more than one brand-new car come back from a demonstration ride on the wrecker's hook, and some of the damage involved was extensive.

If you suspect that your new car has been repainted—if the finish is rough to the touch, if it smells funny, if there's sanding dust in the vents, if there's overspray, if there's an odd piece of painted masking tape that just happens to match the exterior color lying on the floor—stop right there and get someone knowledgeable to look at what you have. You might be looking at the handiwork of someone other than the factory.

Of course, this raises a question: Is the dealer obligated to disclose damage to a buyer? In some states, yes; in some states, no. You might want to check the rules in your state just so you know if you're protected by law.

THE "DEALER TRADE"

One of the facts of life for the import dealer is the *dealer trade*. When the system operates as it should, it allows cooperating dealers to share their inventory and better serve the needs of their customers. Import dealers, typically, have a problem keeping their inventories balanced; even if they have the model in stock that you're after, chances are you can't stand the color. Hence, the dealer trade.

The main problem with dealer trades is the attitude of the

dealer who has the unit the selling dealer needs. If you and I are dealers and you call me on the phone and ask if I have a such and such in gray, and I have two of them, perhaps one that's been repaired and one that's just off the truck, which one do you suppose your customer is going to end up with? If I have a car that doesn't run just right, if I have a car that's been demonstrated to death, if I have a car I've removed parts from to fix a customer's car, which one would I want to send to the dealer who needs the model in gray?

In addition, suppose I suspect that you've made your deal with a customer one of my salesmen was attempting to sell. Could I possibly be just a tad jealous?

Then there is the matter of the physical trade itself. Most trades happen at the end of the month. And what does that mean to the subminimum wage individual who is transferring your new car—at hyperspeed, no doubt—from one dealer to another? He's in a hurry to get back so he can make his next run (most of these drivers are paid by the run and not by the hour).

Things can and do go wrong when people start moving cars around in haste. Should I tell you about the dealer principal who drove a new model back to his dealership from an auto show without any coolant in the radiator? Should I tell you which unlucky salesman sold that unit?

I'd better not.

Instead, let's identify some things for you to look for and be aware of pertaining to your new car at time of delivery or, in the best case, before.

COMMON AREAS FOR SHIPPING DAMAGE

THE LOWER EDGES OF THINGS

Run your hand along the bottom lip of the front and rear bumpers and the front spoiler if there is one. These are expensive to replace and are vulnerable to loading ramps as well as the service department's lifts. They're also sometimes the first clue to more extensive undercarriage damage. Also, don't forget the bottom edges of the doors, hood, and trunk, or anywhere there's a closure. I've seen more than one trunk slammed on a tire iron, or door on the tang of a seatbelt. It also helps to look at a car from a distance. It's surprising what you'll miss if all you do is stand right next to a car as you inspect it.

HORIZONTAL SURFACES

Cars are secured to transporters by chains. These chains are removed, and sometimes dropped, before cars can be removed from the ramps. Look for "dimples," especially on the hood and deck lid of the trunk. These can be hard to spot, especially if the paint isn't broken.

VERTICAL SURFACES

Bend over and sight down the sides of the car. The average new car gets at least as much exposure to door dings while it's on the dealer's lot as it will get at the local supermarket. Use reflections to help you spot surface irregularities. While you're down there, look at the sidewalls of the tires— both sides—if you didn't before.

LENSES AND LIGHTS

If the car has flip-up-type headlights, open them. Some headlights on new models are incredibly expensive, and the vast majority of buyers who take delivery of their new cars during daylight hours never look to see if they are even in their sockets. If a headlight looks dark or slightly smoky in appearance, it's probably bad. Why find out on the way home? Turn it on and see. Also, taillight lenses are annoyingly fragile and can set you back significantly; look at them with care. Once your new car is off the lot, you have zero recourse.

ALIGNMENT OF BODY WORK

Most manufacturers are highly automated; no body shop is. This means that one of the most reliable methods of detecting body repair has to do with the alignment of the individual panels. Look at the clearances on the same panels on the left and right sides of the car. Give special attention to the hood and trunk. How about exterior trim? Does anything catch as the doors are opened and closed?

GLASS AND MOLDINGS

What you're looking for here isn't so much broken glass as imperfections. Many windshields are bonded in at the factory and become part of the actual structural integrity of the car, so if you spot messy globs of black sealer or loose and ill-fitting window trim, it is something to consider.

Also, manufacturers guarantee their windows against leakage. If an outside vendor has repaired your car, you may have to look to him for warranty responsibility.

PAINT

As a salesman, I hated paint. As a service manager, I had nightmares about it. The problem is, the manufacturers have taken a very fragile medium and have attempted to use it to protect a very durable material.

Most new cars need a two-hour, professional cleaning before delivery, and that's only if they're perfect to begin with. And yet, dealers routinely attempt to hire nonprofessional cleanup people. This is exactly why we need to talk about paint.

The typical import car spends a great deal of its time outside, exposed to the elements, until you come along and put it safely away in your garage. This means that if anything is floating around out there, it will probably end up on your paint. Acid rain, or industrial fallout, is a real problem for the auto industry as a whole, and a problem no one has effectively solved.

It looks like a bad case of water spotting, only these water spots won't come off. They go right through to the metal, and the only thing a dealer can do, if he has the time before delivery or if you force him to after the fact, is paint the entire car. Factories have been known to recall cars with acid rain damage and even pay dealers' warranty claims on them. But that doesn't help you if you take delivery of one your dealer is trying to slip through.

As is true of any inspection of paint work, make sure you see the car in good light and make sure the car is dry. One of the favorite tricks for delivering a car with marginal paint is to hand it to the customer dripping wet. You tend to focus on the water droplets instead of the actual painted surfaces. You may hear a lot of excuses—"We're so busy at the end of the month we didn't have time to dry it off," or "It's just out of the detail bay and so it's wet," or "Gee, it was a little dusty so I hosed it off for you"—but stick to your guns. Acid rain damage is easy to spot, but you must see the car dry to know what you're looking at.

Look for surface scratches, too. No one in the world can clean a dark-colored car and not leave the odd scratch here and there. And, of course, light-colored cars have them, too; they're just less apparent. (If you don't believe me, just park any car of your choice under a fluorescent light and look closely.) But there are scratches and then there are *scratches*. If you have a dark car with noticeable and offensive scratches, keep one thing in mind: if the dealership's detail men put that car out looking as if it had been rubbed down with steel wool, they might not have the talent to fix it. You might not want them to attempt to fix the damage; they might make the problem worse. If you just have to have the car, drive it to a professional and take your chances there. There are independent detail men you can find if you make the rounds of the full-service car washes. You might want one to simply look at the car first, if the damage is really bad.

IF IT'S BEEN A DEMONSTRATOR

Demonstrators are used cars. In many cases they've been used hard, maintained not at all, and are in the possession of someone who is driving them for free.

If you buy a demonstrator, you must realize that you are looking at a legitimate used car. Look at everything you ordinarily would on a used car, from tires to engine leaks, from service records to the condition of the trunk. Assume nothing and find out what remains of the factory warranty. A well-kept secret is that if a car has been registered as a demonstrator with the factory it qualifies for a free extended warranty. Policies and qualifications differ somewhat among manufacturers, but if you can wangle accurate documentation about the actual in-service date of your unit, you can always call the distributor for the facts. The customer service departments of the major manufacturers' distributors are uniformly interested in your satisfaction. Be aware of them and use them to your advantage.

THE "EXECUTIVE" CAR OR
"SPECIAL-PURCHASE" CAR

We've talked about the real concern manufacturers have for selling damaged cars to the public at large. We've talked

about some of the very aggressive policies they have on what
a dealer is authorized to repair and then retail. What we
haven't talked about is what happens to the cars that are
returned to the distributor because of excessive damage, or
critical area damage.

Guess what—they aren't all crushed into end tables.

Most of the distributors maintain a fleet of cars that are
driven by various employees, usually but not exclusively management employees. When these cars have a nominal amount
of mileage on them they are offered to the dealers at special
prices, and if the current supply situation is a little on the
short side, as it usually is, these cars are readily purchased.

These cars are classified as used cars. No warranty is
made about whether or not they have been repaired. The
manufacturer is not representing these cars from a primary
position. Sometimes returned units end up in this group.

Let's not get too paranoid, though. I've seen some cars
returned to the distributor that had really inconsequential
damage; cars I would have bought myself, knowing exactly
what the situation was. So don't just automatically turn
down an "executive car" or a "special-purchase" car. Simply
be aware of the possibility of damage and look them over
with care.

THE MOST COMMON PROBLEM AREAS
DEALERS MISS

Let's assume that you have a perfectly normal deal going:
no unusual problems with the car, no unusual problems with
financing or anything else. What, exactly, constitutes "usual"?
What are some things that might go wrong at time of delivery?
And what are the best ways to deal with them?

SOMETHING WON'T WORK

Confidential reports I've seen indicate that 30 to 40 percent of all new cars have some problem at time of delivery.

This includes import cars, cars rated in the top categories in owner satisfaction. Three to four out of every ten delivered—consider that.

How could this be? Don't the dealers inspect their cars before they hand them over to the customer? Isn't there a predelivery inspection required by all of the manufacturers?

Absolutely. But this is the end of the month, remember? Not only is the cleanup department buried under an impossible work load, the technicians suddenly have twice as much work as they can handle. Shortcuts are the order of the day. Unfortunately, the last line of defense between the operational quality of your new car and you is your salesman, but the cleanup department often makes sure that your car isn't ready for him to inspect until after you've already arrived at the dealership for delivery.

The most productive thing you can do, therefore, is to assume that something won't be right on your new car. If it has power windows, run them all up and down. If it has a radio, play it. If it has air-conditioning, even if it's the dead of winter, crank it up. Open and close all of the doors, trunk, and hood. (If the hood and trunk are hard to open or close, look carefully at the roof of your car. When desperate, dealers have been known to switch hoods and trunks with other units in order to get rid of those damaged by acid rain.) In short, operate everything, or count on having to come back. It shouldn't be your responsibility, granted; but you may be the only one with the time to do it, and you certainly have the best reason.

Will the salesman stand still and let you do your thing, while his peers are happily selling cars out from under him? He won't like it, and his manager won't, either, but it's your right to inspect what you're paying for. A good rule of thumb is the faster your salesman wants to go, the slower you go and the closer you look.

One thing you can do to make things more pleasant and far less stressful is to schedule your delivery during an off-peak time during the day. Simply ask the salesman when his slow time is. Tell him, up front, that you like to look your new cars over, thoroughly, at time of delivery. There are a number of hidden benefits to both these tactics. Not only will your salesman make a special effort to inspect your car ahead of time, but the cleanup people will be put on notice to be extra careful and extra thorough.

THE PAPERWORK WON'T BE RIGHT

Another area in which dealers try to save money is in their office help. Often the legal and financial aspects of your transaction are handled by people with no experience whatsoever in either field.

Bring your reading glasses and pay attention to the most mundane details of your paperwork. Is your name spelled correctly on the registration documents? Is the identification number indicated on your paperwork actually the same as the one on your car? If you did use dealer financing, is the payment you expected actually mentioned on the contract? Interest rate? Term? Don't just assume it's all correct. And one other thing: if you do find a mistake, don't automatically assume it was done on purpose.

One of the most intelligent things you can do is to take delivery during office business hours. If you insist on taking delivery on a weekend or late in the evening, who's going to make the corrections on your paperwork? Do you really want to hand over your money and get inaccurate paperwork in return?

THE LAST DEMO RIDE

Finally, insist on driving your new car, one more time, even if you're taking spot delivery (one hopes you aren't), before you sign the papers. This time listen for rattles or unusual noises. Pay close attention to steering and braking performance. Take note of anything that might be unusual in the vehicle's operation. Be assured, in most cases, that your car has been driven since you saw it last. Anything in the world could have happened to it.

Be aware of the fact that this is the point in your purchase when you have the most power. Virtually everyone in the sales structure is eager to consummate the deal. If you've timed yourself correctly, both the office and the service department are open and available. If something is wrong, if you have a legitimate problem, this is the time you'll come the closest to getting it rectified on the spot.

Remember that first date? Did you want that good-night kiss when you got to the front porch? Did either of you say, "Come back next Thursday?"

Not likely.

▪ 11

SHADES OF GRAY

The American College Dictionary defines the word *audacity* as: 1. boldness or daring, esp. reckless boldness. 2. effrontery or insolence.

I would have defined it as the dominant character trait of the typical "gray market" buyer. Let's face it, in order to satisfy either his overdeveloped urge to own something exclusive or his overdeveloped sense of greed, or both, this individual runs the gauntlet of discouraging federal regulations, the very tangible ire of the auto manufacturers and distributors, the barbs and hooks of the get-rich-quick "importers" and DOT/EPA (Department of Transportation/Environmental Protection Agency) certifiers, and the very real possibility that there will be no buyer for the toy in question when its novelty has finally worn off. There are, quite literally, enough things to go wrong in this scheme to provide the plot for an automotive soap opera well into the next century.

But the fact remains, in 1985 (a banner year, admittedly) well over 66,000 cars entered this country through the gray market. This figure represents more cars than some full-fledged manufacturers managed to bring in through their authorized distributors. What exists has the potential to develop into a "gray market for the masses," and not just be the venue of the occasional, well-heeled enthusiast who wants to have a little something his friends don't.

Why such growth and popularity? Money, of course. What other carrot could there be to explain this phenomenon?

THE RATIONALE OF THE GRAY MARKET

The fact is, any manufacturer is going to get whatever he can for his product in any given market. If he can get the crazy Americans to pay $10,000 more for a Mercedes-Benz 450SL than he can in Belgium or West Germany, then that's exactly what he's going to do. It's called good business, especially if you own stock in Mercedes-Benz. I don't have a quarrel with this. What I *do* have a quarrel with is the position the unsuspecting consumer is put into when he enters the gray market without knowing what he's up against. What I'd like to do for you is lift up one corner of the veil that covers this alternative market and show you a few of the things you'll be faced with both before and after you're driving around in your new, freshly "federalized" Euro-screamer; then, if you proceed, at least you've been warned.

Let's begin by laying some of the European groundwork.

Automobiles, in general, are very highly taxed in most European countries. We complain about sales tax when it adds another thousand dollars to our total price. Suppose you had to pay a special "car tax" on top of this figure, and then a *VAT* (value-added tax) to boot? In some European countries, aggressive taxation can double the cost of a new car before the happy owner is out polluting the atmosphere on his own.

Now enter the typical European Mercedes-Benz, Jaguar, BMW, or Volvo dealership. As a rule, these dealers sell their less expensive models a good deal more easily than their expensive models. Given a less affluent customer base, aggravated by high taxes, there just isn't a particularly strong market for the upscale models. And yet, in order to keep the flow of salable units coming in, the dealer has to accept his share of the harder-to-sell units as well. He has a problem, but a problem the gray market entrepreneur can solve.

The gray market importer becomes the classic middleman in this routine. He buys his goods in a weak market, at discount, in some cases very near dealer cost, and brings them to a strong market, still able to undercut the traditional distributors by a significant amount, while making a tidy profit for himself. The European dealer's problem is neatly solved, the gray market importer has made his profit, the ultimate buyer of the car saves thousands of dollars to boot. Altogether a great deal for everyone involved, supposedly.

The theory is sound. The problem lies in the execution.

THE LITTLE-KNOWN "CATCH-22" OF THE DOT/EPA

You must realize that the safety and emission regulations in the United States differ greatly from those of the European countries. This is the major reason most manufacturers produce separate "domestic" and "export" versions of their cars. When you bring in one of the European spec cars, certain things must be done to it to make it conform. This is one joker in the deck that causes more than its share of trouble for the unwary.

There are two government agencies that are reponsible for automobiles in this country, exclusive of the import process. The Environmental Protection Agency, primarily interested in emissions control, and the Department of Transportation, mostly concerned about adherence to federally mandated safety regulations. These are the watchdogs the American public depends on to ensure that we drive safe cars, at least from a basic design standpoint, and cars that don't destroy our ecology. In theory, these agencies ensure that any car allowed through customs is up to standards, or else not allowed to be licensed for operation.

But, neither the EPA nor the DOT inspects cars directly. Instead, for automobiles imported outside regular channels, they license conversion laboratories to make any required alterations and install any required equipment. Then these two steadfast protectors of the public simply take the word of the privately run conversion facilities that the work has been done properly. Still no problem, if it weren't for one last detail: *not only are the specific cars not inspected, neither the EPA nor the DOT routinely inspects the conversion facilities they have licensed.* It's a lot like hiring the fox to watch your chickens—and then going on vacation.

This means that you can do everything required by all government agencies involved, make a conscientious effort to conform to the very letter of the law, and still end up having your car confiscated at a later date because the Department of Motor Vehicles accidentally discovers that your "converter" failed to do a complete job on your car.

Are you qualified to open up the hood on your BMW M-1 and tell if the little black box that controls your emissions is programmed correctly? Do you expect to take off your interior door panels to see if the steel beams that protect you against side impact have been installed properly? Could you crawl under your car and tell me what your catalytic converter looks like? Could you tell me if it's the right one for your car? Even if you can do all of these things, how many other people do you think can? How would you like to pay $3,000 to $5,000 for a conversion, find out later that your certifications had been falsified, and have to do it all over again with another lab, because your original converter was long gone?

And falsifying certifications is a big business. How many cars would you have to certify at $5,000 a crack before you could leave the country as a very wealthy individual?

Even the General Accounting Office (GAO) has become

alarmed. Recently, the GAO has said publicly that the rules governing gray market imports are not strict enough and that the current system has insufficient checks against fraud. And much to the credit of the GAO, federal prosecutors have begun to turn their attention to the problem.

But it's too late for a lot of people. In fact, as the fraudulent labs are exposed, hundreds of these labs' past customers are going to get a nasty surprise. Either they're going to have to get their cars refederalized, or they're going to lose them.

THE ACCORDION EFFECT

Even with the plight of the European dealer and the discount available because of the different pricing structure, there has been another, probably more important, set of circumstances to fuel the rapid growth of the gray market. Since about 1981 the dollar has steadily gained strength on the world market. At its peak in 1985 the dollar commanded 3.09 deutsche marks in exchange for every single dollar. In simple terms this meant more European car for less money. At the same time, however, the manufacturers saw fit not to reduce their prices for the American market in line with the world monetary market. Instead, they chose to take advantage of this "invisible price increase" and put themselves in a very happy profit-taking mode. They should have known there would be repercussions.

By December 1985, there were thirty-seven different companies advertising either gray market importing, converting, or consulting in *Autoweek*. Assuredly, several hundred more "privateers" operated on a referral-only basis. For people with easy access to Europe and the desire to make a lot of money quickly, this became a favored method. For instance, as a salesman I met more than one airline pilot who had a lucrative business going on the side, and I was approached by more than one of them to "point" a few likely prospects in their direction, which, admittedly with many second thoughts, I declined.

By mid-1986, however, the dollar had fallen by nearly a third and the flow of gray market cars was down by more than half, to approximately thirty thousand units. Still a far cry from the two thousand units that came into the country in 1981, but the accordion had collapsed in a hurry, squeezing a lot of the small operations out of the business. In addition, federal prosecutors opened their eyes, and fraudulent converters started to go to jail on a regular basis. In *Autoweek*, less than a year and a half after the market's high-water mark, the number of converters, importers, and consultants still advertising was less than half a dozen, total. By the first quarter of 1987 the number had dwindled to three. Of course, there are a good many more people involved in the business than the ones who happen to advertise in *Autoweek*, but I think the power of the example is clear. A good many of the converters, importers, and consultants just aren't around anymore.

One assumption we ordinarily make when we buy a car from a major manufacturer—such as Porsche, BMW, Mercedes-Benz, or Volvo—is that the company will be there when we want to have our car serviced or warranty work performed. With the gray market car you have no such guarantee, and don't think the factory will take pity on you and authorize warranty repairs. You didn't buy your car from their authorized distributor, remember? And the dealer couldn't care less if your gray market BMW won't idle properly, or if your gray market Mercedes suddenly can't pass its emissions test.

And what if you finally get tired of your clandestinely imported car and decide to trade it in on a U.S. spec version? Will the dealer welcome you with open arms?

THE BLACK AND WHITE OF TRADING GRAYS

We've already talked about the wholesale market in used cars. At this point you're well aware of the important role the wholesale auction plays in the redistribution of trade-ins to their most appropriate dealers. Imagine that a whole classification of cars was barred from even being entered in a wholesale auction. What would happen to the value of these cars that couldn't be wholesaled in the normal way?

Feeling queasy? If you currently own a gray market car of any description you should be, for there is an unwritten law at the wholesale auction level that no gray market cars be accepted into the sale. The auctioneers, it seems, are worried that they might inadvertently become part of the "distribution chain" of these cars, and they want to avoid any possible exposure to the massive liability potentials of improperly federalized gray market cars. Something to think about when you go to sell one of these cars yourself, isn't it?

So, how does a dealer place a value on a gray market trade-in? Usually, they start at half the current wholesale listed for the U.S.-market model and go from there. That is, if they consider taking the car in trade at all.

WHAT THE MANUFACTURERS ARE ATTEMPTING TO DO ABOUT THE GRAY MARKET AND WHAT THEY HAVE TO LOSE IF THEY'RE UNSUCCESSFUL

The manufacturers are up in arms over the entire gray market issue, which might seem confusing because they've made a sale either way. Why would Mercedes-Benz care if one of the cars it had actually manufactured for sale in Europe ends up in the United States, anyway? The company was paid just the same, wasn't it?

Yes and no. The U.S. distributor must pay more for his cars than his European counterpart. This means loss of revenue for the manufacturer. And it also means something else just as important: loss of control over the quality of the manufacturer's product.

Why do the major European manufacturers enjoy such a strong marketing position in this country in the first place? Engineering, product performance, reliability, fit and finish—in short, quality. The gray market importer has no stake in the long-term future of the individual manufacturer's products. When the money market makes his endeavor unprofitable he'll simply find a new angle. The manufacturer must live with every disappointed owner, no matter what. The bottom line for long-term success in this country or any other is owner satisfaction, and this is a major reason the manufacturers would like to see the gray market curtailed or possibly even legislated out of existence altogether.

Lacking direct control of Congress, however, most manufacturers have embarked on an aggressive program that includes strongly discouraging the European dealer from doing business with known gray market importers, issuing equally strong warnings to the U.S dealer network not to participate in either new or used grays, withholding warranty assistance on gray market cars even though world warranties should conceivably apply, offering more of the "European" models through normal channels, and trying to bring U.S.-spec models up to European-model performance standards. (This perhaps is made easier by the impact of new lead-free fuel and emissions awareness in Europe.)

Only one thing is certain in the manufacturer's view: the gray market problem is sure to resurface again and again with the fluctuations of the world money market. Manufacturers have no choice but to meet the problem head-on.

A PROMISE KEPT

In the very beginning of this book I promised you only a brief discussion of the gray market issue. There is, of course, a tremendous amount of additional material to be covered beside what we've touched on. Regulations are sure to change in the near future; manufacturers are sure to develop new ways to deal with the problem. Any detailed analysis of the gray market issue would quite likely be obsolete in the very near future. But we have taken a look at some of the basic concepts and basic pitfalls involved in circumventing the normal import channels. The one point I hope I have successfully made is that when you eliminate the authorized distributor/ dealer network you also eliminate many of the safeguards you've probably always taken for granted.

If you'd truly like to save a little money on a European car, and you'd like to see the Continent in the bargain, there is an alternative—one that's so safe you might find it boring.

EUROPEAN DELIVERY

There is a way, unspectacular though it might be, to save $1,000 or more on the purchase of a fully legal American-spec European car, especially if you're in the market for one of the more expensive models or one of the extremely hard-to-find variations that tend to show up in the showroom with a large premium or "availability surcharge" attached. This, of course, is the factory-authorized European Delivery Program (EDP) available through virtually all of the major European manufacturers.

WHY THE DEALER LIKES EUROPEAN DELIVERY

In a word: *allocation*. There is no limit to the number of cars a Stateside dealer can sell on European Delivery. There's also no floor plan to pay, no worries about a car's being improperly detailed or damaged on the lot. To the dealer it's free money. You give him your money, then you go get your car somewhere else.

You may have to twist your salesperson's arm to tell you

about the program—he'll naturally want to sell you a car out of his stock so he can get paid sooner on the deal. But if you persevere you'll find someone who will clue you in and take your deposit. (This is one time when it's probably a good idea to shop the dealer in an off-peak period. If the dealership doesn't do much of this sort of business, the people you're dealing with might have to figure out the program first. But don't worry about this; the manufacturer supplies the dealer with an explicit manual.)

PRICING

Here's something you'll really like, especially those of you who can't stand to negotiate. The factory publishes a price list for the cars sold on their EDP. Not only is this price a good deal lower than the ordinary manufacturers' suggested retail price, you won't find the mention of a surcharge or a premium or a dealer-prep charge anywhere on it. Immediately you have access to a better deal than you could ever negotiate on a car in the dealer's inventory. The best part is, you don't have to stop there. If a European Delivery car means free money to one dealer, it means the same thing to any other dealer. Why not drop a hint that you might just like a better deal? I worked for one dealer who would openly suggest that he would further discount the car in order to secure the order. Why not? Especially if the dealer involved has a small allocation.

Would you like to take that European vacation you've always dreamed about and come home with a new car at a discount price to boot? Buy a car normally sold well over sticker and you can come out way ahead.

FINANCING

Finance your European Delivery car the same way you would finance any other car. All the bank needs is documentation that says they will be on the title, and proof of insurance coverage. Some banks will readily lease these vehicles. Some manufacturers can help you even further: Volvo, for instance, owns its own leasing entity and will be more than happy to lease you a Volvo for European Delivery.

TIME FRAMES

Most manufacturers require six to eight weeks to ensure that they'll have the exact car you want when you show up on their doorstep. However, I've done it for people in less than thirty days when they weren't locked in on a particular color or exact equipment list. This was possible because most manufacturers keep a "pool" of U.S.-spec models on hand at their tourist delivery centers just for the last-minute buyer. The motto here is, if you're short on time, it never hurts to take a shot. Have your salesman, or his manager, check the pool before you give up on the idea completely.

INSURANCE

The Europeans are very picky about their insurance regulations. You will be required to purchase special insurance in order to obtain the special registration documents you will need. But all of the EPD programs offer this as part of their packages. Your premiums will vary according to how long you plan to stay in Europe. Unfortunately, thirty days' worth of insurance is the minimum, even if you plan to dash across for just a few days.

CONFIRMATION

You must have written confirmation from the factory that your order has been accepted and will be filled. They know how many cars they have left to build in any given model, and unlike the dealer, they have nothing to gain by selling you a car they know they can't deliver. Don't assume that just because you have ordered the car directly from the factory it will automatically be available. Wait for confirmation before you set your travel plans in concrete.

Also, don't place multiple orders for cars from different manufacturers just to cover yourself. Your car will be paid for in advance. If you default, these people will keep a chunk of your money for their trouble.

SHIPPING ARRANGEMENTS

Cars shipped from the factory are usually shipped free, which makes this your best bet. But if you can't drop off the car where you picked it up, cars are routinely shipped from most major European ports. As a matter of fact, if you make the arrangements in advance, shipping can be arranged from virtually anyplace on the Continent. I recommend you drop off the car yourself, if not back at the factory, at least at the port. You'll save a good deal of money and have much less exposure to damage.

At this end, expect to pick up your car at one of the major U.S. ports (you'll be asked to designate which one). If you live in the Midwest, or anyplace where this will be impractical, you'll have to make special arrangements to have your car transported inland. A word to the wise: going after it yourself is usually less expensive and a better idea.

CATALYTIC CONVERTERS

There's a growing trend in Europe toward unleaded fuel and catalytic converters for the same reasons we have gone to them in this country, but unless you are told differently by the technician who delivers your car to you, count on seeing your catalytic converter lying in your trunk when you first get your car. Don't despair; your price automatically included the reinstallation of this device prior to shipping.

One tip: fuel is expensive in Europe, so don't return your car to the dropoff point with a full tank of fuel. Also, if you have been burning leaded fuel while you were in Europe, you must drain this fuel out and replace it before operating your car Stateside or you will damage your converter. Save yourself some trouble and make a dead-stick landing back at the factory or at the port. A gallon or two left in the tank is all that is required for the shippers' purposes.

PICKING IT UP AT THE PORT

Have a friend who's good at spotting dents and scratches? Take him to the port to pick up your car. You'll need a ride anyway, and no claim will be honored by the shipping company if you fail to note the damage before you drive off their property.

THE QUESTION OF THE TRADE-IN

You are going to beat your car back from Europe by several weeks, depending on the specific shipping schedules. Ask yourself what you'll drive back and forth to work while your new car is enjoying a leisurely ocean voyage. If you need your car, keep it until the new one arrives. If not, pretrade it to the dealer; that is, let him have your car for whatever credit you've negotiated just before leaving for Europe. You'll save a small amount of depreciation this way and, more important, you'll avoid the pitfalls of a reappraisal when you get back from your trip.

THE APPROVED METHOD OF GLOATING
AFTER THE FACT

Take lots of pictures while you're in Europe, making sure your new car is featured in the majority of your shots. Let your friends know that your European vacation was "free."

IN CONCLUSION

I read somewhere once that if you never want to make mistakes or feel uncomfortable, never do anything for the first time. A true statement, I'm sure, but what a pathetic way to go through life. Dealing with salesmen, comparison-shopping, forcing yourself to do a little financial planning and figuring—all of these things are going to challenge you and force you to grow a bit, but they will be worth it in the long run. Just think how much money you'll save on your next new car if you can successfully apply what you've learned in this book. Just think how much you can save on every remaining car you purchase as you get better and better at the game.

I hope you're motivated. I hope you make the effort. It will certainly be worth your while if you do.

Remember this final thought: you, too, can buy an import car with good humor, with a minumum of frustration, and without having to lie to anyone or do anything that might compromise your values. Buying a car can and should be good, clean fun—and profitable at the same time! To be a winner, all you really have to do is get the facts and then play your cards carefully.

And wouldn't I like to be there to see you pull it off.

174